FRONTIER TRAILS
The Autobiography of
FRANK M. CANTON

A BUFFALO-HUNTERS' CAMP

FRONTIER TRAILS

The Autobiography of

FRANK M. CANTON

EDITED BY

EDWARD EVERETT DALE

WITH ILLUSTRATIONS

BOSTON AND NEW YORK

HOUGHTON MIFFLIN COMPANY

The Riverside Press Cambridge

1930

The Riverside Press
CAMBRIDGE · MASSACHUSETTS
PRINTED IN THE U.S.A.

PREFACE

Soon after his death in 1927 the private papers of General Frank M. Canton were deposited with the University of Oklahoma for safe-keeping. Among these papers were found five thick notebooks in which Canton had written the story of his life. It is impossible to say exactly when this life story was written, but there is evidence that it must have been done in 1908 or 1909, soon after Canton had been appointed Adjutant General of the Oklahoma National Guard.

The material seemed of unusual interest and work was soon begun on the task of preparing it for publication. In offering the volume to the reading public the editor wishes to acknowledge his indebtedness to General Canton's widow, Mrs. F. M. Canton, of Edmond, Oklahoma, not only for the manuscript and permission to publish it, but also for much information with respect to the author's early life and work. The editor also wishes to express his thanks to his wife, Rosalie Gilkey Dale, whose assistance in arranging and typing the manuscript, as well as in choosing illustrations and in reading proof, has been invaluable.

EDWARD EVERETT DALE

NORMAN, OKLAHOMA
January 15, 1930

CONTENTS

ILLUSTRATIONS

INTRODUCTION

IN the picturesque drama of settling and developing the Great West the frontier peace officer has played a leading part. Often a quiet, unassuming man, he stood as the representative of law and order in a region where many people cared little for either. Theoretically he was supported by all the power of organized government. Practically, he stood all too often alone at his post of duty, a solitary sentinel whose efficiency and even life itself must depend upon his own personal resources of cool determination and quickness and skill in the use of arms.

A citizen-soldier, he had all the perils and hardships and but few of the advantages that came to the man in the uniform of the regular army. The enemy was always near at hand. Every day had its dangers, since the war against crime and criminals never ceased. No retirement allowances were his, regardless of how long he had served. If disabled in the line of duty, no government hospital stood ready to receive him, and if 'killed in action,' no pension came to his widow and children.

The apparent injustice of such a system did not turn these men aside from their chosen work. Strong, alert, and fearless, they fought and won the battles of law against anarchy, of right against might, and eventually made life and property in the West secure for the pioneer home-builder and his family.

With the death of General Frank M. Canton, in

1927, passed one of the most picturesque and efficient
of the veteran peace officers of the American frontier.
For more than fifty years Canton served society as
Texas Ranger, United States Deputy Marshal, live-
stock inspector, sheriff, and secret-service man. His
trail stretched from the Rio Grande to the Arctic
Ocean, and his colorful life was one long adventure.

In justice to the reader as well as to the memory of
the writer of this life story, it seems well to state that
the author's real name was not Frank Canton. In his
youth he became involved in a difficulty that caused
him to leave his Texas home and disappear into the
farther depths of the American wilderness. Here he
took the name of Frank M. Canton, and made it
honored and respected throughout the length and
breadth of a vast region.

Many years later, when this buried chapter of his
past was resurrected, this early difficulty was adjusted
and Mr. Canton absolved from all blame in connection
with it. Some of his friends and relatives then urged
him to assume once more his real name, but he refused.
He had, in the mean time, married. He had a host of
friends who knew him only as Frank Canton, while
there remained but little to connect him with this
remote past of his boyhood days.

So as Frank M. Canton he lived, adding to the name
year by year fresh luster, until 1907 when, as a culmina-
tion to his many honors, he was appointed Adjutant
General of the National Guard of Oklahoma by Charles
N. Haskell, first Governor of that State.

He served in this capacity for nine years and under three governors. Failing health at last caused him to retire a short time before the entrance of the United States into the Great War, a struggle in which he eagerly desired to have an active part, but age and ill-health made it impossible.

For some years after the close of the war, he lived quietly with his family at the little town of Edmond, Oklahoma, located near the center of the State to which he had rendered such long and signal service.

His real name does not matter. As Frank M. Canton his memory is honored, not only in Oklahoma, but throughout all that wide region reaching from the Mexican Border to Cape Nome, and from the Mississippi River to the Rockies and far beyond.

Many of his old-time friends and companions have passed away, but not a few still linger who knew and loved him. In almost any part of the Great West where the old pioneers gather to fight their old battles over again and tell tall tales of the early days, the name of Frank Canton will still cause faded old eyes to brighten, while quavering voices relate wonderful stories of their former comrade — this veteran frontier peace officer whose restless feet traveled so many of the frontier trails of Western America.

FOREWORD BY THE AUTHOR

I HAVE served more than fifty years as an officer on the Western frontier. My chief duty has been to protect the good citizens from the bad men who infested the border settlements in the early days. In this capacity I have worked from the Rio Grande to the Red River in Texas, and from there to the Yukon in Alaska. My experiences have included about everything in the line of outlaw fighting. I have had to deal with the Mexican Greaser, the Indian, and all classes of white criminals, such as train robbers, stage robbers, horse thieves, and cattle thieves.

I have been requested frequently of late years to write an autobiography. I have virtually done this when I narrate the incidents of my official life during these fifty years.

It is needless for me to state that what I shall write in this life story will be the plain, uncolored truth. It will contain no fiction. I do not feel that it is necessary to draw on the creative imagination of the novelist to make a story of this character more interesting; besides, no writer of fiction could think of the plots that a country full of outlaws would invent for the man that was chasing them; neither could he think of and describe the many kinds of narrow escapes and thrilling adventures that would happen to the sheriff who put in a lifetime as an officer during these pioneer times, and was fortunate enough to come out with a whole skin.

I was born in Virginia, fifteen miles from the city of Richmond, in 1849. My parents moved to Denton County in northern Texas when I was a child. The Great Lone Star State in the late sixties was in a fierce struggle with the various elements of outlawry. At that time there were but few settlements west of what is now the city of Fort Worth, which was then a little frontier village, with hostile bands of Indians scouting near its limits. It is a great city now, one of the largest railroad centers in the South; but at that time there was no railroad within hundreds of miles.

Over the west two thirds of the State, which was one great rolling prairie, roamed countless thousands of wild cattle and wilder buffalo. Here they were free to graze, unrestrained by barbed wire, over the finest grass land in the world. Here was the natural home of the cow, the land of the cowboy, and the paradise of the desperado.

I have mentioned these conditions in order to give my readers some idea of the environment of my early boyhood days. From the time that I was old enough to climb into a saddle, I was riding over the range. My associates were cowboys, and from them I learned to use the rope. I also absorbed many ideas about the cattle business, such as the handling of the big herds when taking them over the trails. Many cattle were being moved at that time from Texas to western Kansas and Nebraska. This country at that time, like

Texas, was a big belt of prairie, fringed on the Rocky Mountain side with sagebrush. Oklahoma was in a wild and unsettled condition.

I was now a boy of seventeen. I was eager to join in one of these big cattle drives to the northwest. Just what would make a trip of that kind so inviting, even to an ambitious boy who craved excitement, I am unable to say. But when you are on the border, there is a certain lure which draws you on farther and still farther. I suppose it is what Jack London would term the 'Call of the Wild.'

FRONTIER TRAILS

FRONTIER TRAILS

·.·

CHAPTER I

UP THE TRAIL

THERE was a young man by the name of Burk Burnett who was one of our neighbors in Denton County. His father, Jerry Burnett, was an old settler and cattleman. In the spring of 1869 Captain M. B. Lloyd, who organized the first bank in Fort Worth, in company with Burk Burnett and his father, got together a herd of fifteen hundred head of cattle to drive to Abilene, Kansas. Burk was then a young, lively cowboy, and he was placed in charge of this herd. He asked me to go with him, saying that I would need four good cow ponies. I agreed to go. It was strictly in line with my wishes for two or three years previous. I got my cow ponies and equipment on the trail with a herd of cattle. I soon found that I had a great deal to learn, but was willing to work, and by close attention managed to do my part in such a manner that I was not called a tenderfoot.

We drove our cattle to the Rock Crossing on Red River which is a short distance above Gainesville, Texas. We found the river was bank full, and this meant that we would have to swim every inch of the way across. To any one who has ever seen the South

Canadian or the Red River on a rampage, this description will seem weak and meager compared to their impressions. These streams have their sources in the great canyons of the Rocky Mountains. The spring rains and thaws, helped out by an occasional waterspout, suddenly fill these canyons with water that goes rolling down out of the mountains onto the river beds of the plains, and the great supply does not exhaust itself until these streams empty into the larger rivers below. These flood waters become mixed with the great bed of quicksand, which makes it difficult for either a man or beast to swim in. It is more than forty years ago, yet I distinctly remember how the old Red River was cutting up on this occasion. The waters were rushing swiftly, carrying uprooted trees and other débris down the current. In places great waves dashing against a sandbar or some shallow place would throw spouting sheets of water into the air. It was indeed a seething maelstrom. I did not wonder that the cattle refused to be driven into this water. For I confess that it did not look safe to try to swim it. Cattle are very hard to drown, and will swim longer than a horse; but sometimes after they get into the water the leaders will turn back and the whole bunch begin to swim in a circle, and the herd will follow the leaders just as they do in a stampede, and this circle must be broken or they will all drown.

Finally we cut off a good bunch of the leaders and drove them into the water. They headed towards the opposite shore, with Tib Burnett, brother of Burk,

swimming ahead of them on his pony. The rest of us
were all working like beavers to drive the herd into the
river before the leaders landed on the opposite side,
but they had got scared and it was impossible to make
them take the water. We worked four days before we
succeeded in getting the entire herd across. We tried
to start them at nearly every curve in the river until
we reached what was known as Spanish Fort Bend
above Gainesville. Here we started the whole herd towards the river, and made the cattle in the rear crowd
the leaders off into the water. One of our cowboys was
ready and leaped in with his horse and started to swim
ahead of the cattle to pilot them across. They began
to follow him and more of the cattle began to jump in,
for now that the leaders had started, they all wanted
to go. In twenty minutes the whole herd was swimming in a straight line for the opposite bank, but the
current was so swift that we landed about a mile
down the river. Our loose horses swam over, and we
made a raft heavy enough to hold up our mess wagon,
which we drifted over safely.

After we had crossed the river we went into camp to
dry out. Tib Burnett, who had crossed over several
days before at the Rock Crossing, had thrown in his
bunch of cattle with another cow outfit, and started on
the trail ahead of us. We did not see him again until
we reached Abilene, Kansas.

The rainy season had set in and we had a hard trip
for the first ten days in the Indian Territory. Electric
storms and heavy rains caused the cattle to commence

stampeding, which kept us in the saddle day and night.
When we had a chance for a little sleep we would drop
down on our wet saddle-blankets and cover with our
slickers. I did not have a dry stitch of clothes on for a
week. We passed near the west slope of the Arbuckle
Mountains, and angled across the country in a north-
westerly direction until we struck the Chisholm Trail.
Since the country we traveled over, which is now western Oklahoma, is settled up so thickly, I cannot locate
just where the trail ran. We did not know the names
of the streams we crossed, and had to swim most of
them. Not a soul lived in the country on our route;
nothing but buffalo, antelope, deer, wild turkey, lobo
wolves, and coyotes. The rainy weather seemed to be
over. The sun came out. Our cattle were now well
broken to the trail and we had a chance to catch up
on sleep. We congratulated ourselves on not having
seen an Indian on the trip. Other outfits ahead of us
had not been so lucky. Many other herds had been
stampeded by Indians and in one instance several
cowboys had been killed. We were getting up pretty
well north in the Indian Territory — I think it was
about twenty miles from the Kansas line. We had
stopped the mess wagon for dinner. A short distance
away was a tall bluff overlooking a small creek. I rode
down near the bluff and dismounted to gather some
wild sand plums, which were the first fruit that I had
seen on the trip. After I had eaten all I wanted and
was filling my hat with some of the most select of the
ripe ones to take back to camp, I looked up and saw

A TRAIL HERD GRAZING

two Indians on a bluff above me about fifty yards away, their faces painted, and wearing gaudy eagle feathers. These things, coupled with the glaring, hateful look which they gave me, made them look hideous indeed. They sat on their horses watching me, and I returned their glance for a few moments, but neither of us said a word. Finally I jumped on my cow pony and spurred him for camp. The two Indians made no attempt to follow me, but disappeared over the hill in another direction.

After I had reported to Burk Burnett what I had seen, we hurried to the wagon and examined what few guns we had and found that they were very rusty from the wet weather and in no condition for service. We had brought along with us some old Henry rifles, which were rim fire and not much good, but we all had good six-shooters with plenty of ammunition. We had scarcely got our guns cleaned and loaded when about twenty-five mounted Indians came galloping down towards the herd. We mounted our horses and began to ride around the cattle so as to bunch them closely. The Indians rode up to us. They and their horses were covered with war paint. Both sides of their heads were shaven, leaving a stiff roach beginning from the forehead in front and extending over the back of their heads. They were fine, kingly looking fellows, and we learned afterwards that they were Osages. Each Indian had a bow and quiver of arrows with steel-tipped heads, and they were also armed with good rifles and apparently had plenty of ammunition. They selected one Indian who could talk broken English and used him as an interpreter. He said that his tribe owned all that country and that they demanded one hundred head of beef cattle for allowing us to drive our herd over their buffalo range. We then held a conference and decided that we could stand off this bunch of twenty-five if it came to a showdown, so Burnett put on a bold front and told their leader that his demand was refused.

About this time war bonnets began to show up all along the horizon. I think about two hundred Indians altogether rode down towards us from the top of the ridge about a quarter of a mile away. When the chief learned that we would not give up the cattle, he made a sign to the Indians and they rode into the herd and killed six head with the bow and arrow, the same as they kill buffalo. As the situation did not look good to us, we made no effort to stop them but commenced to drift our herd to the north. These Indians were in a hateful mood and I have often wondered why they allowed us to escape with our scalps. The worst they did after killing the cattle was to go down to the mess wagon and punch the cook around with their rifles, and take away from him all of our tobacco, some bacon and a lot of other supplies.

Had we known anything about the Indian we might have compromised by giving them ten or fifteen cattle, and this would have saved us many hardships as well as the needless risking of our lives, but this was one of the things that we had to learn.

After the Indians left us, we drove our herd about eight miles farther north and went into camp for the night on the south bank of the Kaw River. After having the cattle bedded down in good shape for the night, we arranged for the detail of night herders. The horse wrangler was directed to take the loose horses away not far from the cattle and herd them for the night. We were not exactly expecting trouble, for we supposed the Indians were satisfied, yet we decided to keep on the watch. Each man picketed one cow pony near the wagon and the rest were all turned loose in the horse herd. We spread our blankets down on the thick buffalo grass and turned in. It was a beautiful moonlight night, with not a sound to be heard except an occasional howl of the lobo wolf, or the quick, short yelp of the coyote. The two night herders kept up a chanting song as they rode back and forth around the herd. This singing seems to have a soothing and quieting effect upon cattle as they are resting for the night. The cattle had plenty of time to graze before we bedded them, and were now all lying down at rest; probably not more than half a dozen in the big herd were standing up.

I think it was about one o'clock in the night when I was awakened from a sound sleep by a deep, rumbling noise of a stampede. This is a sound that the cowboy never mistakes for anything else and always dreads to hear. I sprang to my feet instantly and ran for my horse, saddle and bridle in hand. Burk Burnett had gotten on his feet first, snatched up his bridle, jumped on his horse bareback, without hat, pants, or boots. He was riding like the wind to head off the leaders of the herd. I had saddled my horse and mounting him, I followed Burk at top speed. The cattle were strung out along beside us. Their glistening horns clattered together, making a sound like hail falling on a tin roof as they crowded, snorted, and raced headlong over the prairie. We knew that we could not stop them, but if we could turn the leaders, we would soon have them running in a circle until they would wind themselves up like the coils of a snail shell. I drew up even with Burk, and he caught up with the leaders and was whipping them over the side of the head with his quirt. Finally, we succeeded in turning the leaders until they were following as much as they were leading. They turned and kept on turning and those that followed them also turned, until they were at last brought to a stop. They packed themselves together so tightly that those in the center of the bunch could hardly move. It takes time to tell these things, but from the time we first commenced to turn the lead steers it was not more than five minutes until we had the herd rounded up in a seething mass, so close together that they could not run. Then we quieted them down by singing to them as we circled around the herd. Some of them had their horns broken off, and a few had broken legs, but we had them all anyway.

Some time after the stampede the two night herders came in one at a time from across the prairie and reported that our cattle had been stampeded by the

Indians. The next morning the horse wrangler who was very badly scared showed up with the cheerful news that the Indians had run off our entire herd of saddle horses. The Indians had virtually set us afoot, as we had only the horses that we had picketed out the night before, and these we were compelled to save for night work. There was nothing for us to do but drive on foot in the daytime, as we could not buy horses any place along the trail. Then commenced the hardest trip of my life.

Of course we had to have a rider on either side of them to keep them headed in the right direction, while the rest of us walked. For the first few days the cattle were so afraid of us that we could hardly keep in sight of them. Our footwear was not suitable for walking, as our riding boots with the long pointed heels were so uncomfortable that our feet were soon in solid blisters. We had to dodge rattlesnakes in running over prairie-dog towns and we did not dare take a shot at them for fear of stampeding the cattle. Some of the boys cut holes in their tight-fitting boots to ease their swollen feet, and this gave the small prickly pear a chance to get in its work. Finally the cattle got so hungry that they had to graze and they began to let us get a little closer. We all decided in our own minds that the proper thing to do in the future was to kill and scalp every Indian we met, no matter what tribe he belonged to, just so he was an Indian.

We tramped along in this weary fashion until we came to the Arkansas River, which we crossed at a point which is now Wichita, Kansas. At that time there were only two shacks in the town, one a saloon and the other a small grocery store. Here we came upon Colonel C. C. Slaughter, now a leading banker of Dallas, Texas, who was camped at Wichita with a bunch of cattle. He bought a canteen of whiskey at the saloon and brought it out to camp. That night we had a big storm. Slaughter's cattle stampeded and were so badly scattered that it took him thirty days to round them up again. We held our herd during the storm. Colonel Slaughter afterwards said that the canteen of whiskey cost him three thousand dollars.

We got through to Abilene with our herd in good shape if the herders were not. Captain Lloyd of Fort Worth, and his daughter Ruth, who had been attending school at Topeka, met us at Abilene. We stayed there a few days. The cattle were sold for a good profit, and then we all separated. Burk Burnett, Captain Lloyd and his daughter went back to Texas. I remained at Abilene about a week and then joined another cow outfit with twenty-five hundred head of cattle, owned by Snyder and Kingsbury, to be delivered at North Platte, Nebraska.

There was an immense herd of buffalo on the northwestern plains at that time. The Pawnee Indians claimed the country from the North Platte River to the Arkansas on the south for their hunting grounds, which took in what is now southern Wyoming, eastern Colorado, and western Nebraska and western Kansas. The Sioux and Cheyenne had the country which is now

North and South Dakota and eastern Montana to the Yellowstone River.

The Pawnee Indians at one time were a powerful tribe of the plains, but the Sioux, with the assistance of their ally, the Cheyenne, were too much for the Pawnees and after a bitter and relentless war between the tribes, the Pawnees were almost annihilated and the Sioux were the boss of the plains. The United States Government then gathered up the remnant of the Pawnees and placed them on a reservation in the Indian Territory, which is now Pawnee County, Oklahoma.

When we reached western Nebraska with our herd of cattle, we found that the Sioux Indians were waging a merciless warfare against the Pawnees, but were not on the war path against the whites. One night, while we camped on Big Blue River, our cattle stampeded and the next morning we found that about three hundred head were missing. Three other cowboys and myself were detailed to hunt for the missing cattle. We circled around for about two hours and then struck their trail. The tracks showed that the cattle were headed towards the Platte River. There were unshod pony tracks in the cattle trail and also the tracks of a mule. We knew then that our cattle had been stolen and supposed the thieves were Indians, as they generally ride ponies that are unshod. We followed the trail until we were near the Platte.

It was late in the evening when we rode into a band of about one hundred Sioux Indians who were skinning a number of buffalo that they had just killed. They saw us first and we had no time to conceal ourselves. They rushed up and gathered all around us. To our surprise they appeared to be friendly, and through one of their band who could talk fair English, they began to converse with us. They were armed to the teeth, both with bows and arrows, clean, new rifles and plenty of ammunition. They and their horses were decorated with war paint and eagle feathers, while the absence of women and children showed that they were out for war.

One of them said, 'Who are you, and where are you going?'

After we answered them truthfully, they wanted to know if we had seen any Pawnees over south killing buffalo. We told them that we had seen no Indians. We asked them if they had seen anything of our cattle. They told us that about two hours before they had seen three white men about two miles from there, holding a bunch of cattle at a water-hole. These white men, they said, lived a few miles below our camp on the Big Blue River. The Indians said that these men were 'heap bad, all time steal Indian pony.'

After they had pointed out the direction and the location of where they had last seen the cattle, we gave them some tobacco and left them. I noticed that the green buffalo hides which they had with them all had the horns left on the hide. I thought this rather peculiar but asked no questions.

After we left the Indians we held a conference and

SIOUX INDIANS SKINNING BUFFALO

decided that they had been lying to us. We made up our minds that this was the bunch that had stolen our cattle. One of our party who had been riding ahead jumped off his horse and examining the ground motioned us to come to him. We found the trail of the cattle in the direction that the Indians had pointed out to us with the three pony tracks and also the mule track still following in the trail.

As it was getting too dark to trail the cattle, and for fear of riding into an ambush, we concluded to go into camp. I had cut some fresh buffalo steak from a carcass before leaving the Indians and after building a fire where it could not be seen from the hills, we broiled our steak and ate it without salt. We were all hungry as wolves and it tasted pretty good. After putting the fire out we lay down on our saddle blankets and slept for a few hours until daybreak, when we got up and took the trail again. I was armed with a rifle and six-shooter, while the other boys had revolvers only. After we had gone about two miles I dismounted and crept upon a hill where I could view the surrounding country, and discovered our cattle about a half-mile away. A white man was herding them. The Indians had told us the truth, but I could not see the camp of the other two men. We decided to lead our horses and slip upon the camp, if we could locate it, and capture the two men first. We soon discovered smoke behind a big bluff and knew the camp was there. One of our men, a young fellow by the name of Sam Tate, was crawling along the edge of the bluff leading his horse.

His revolver slipped out of the holster and fell some four feet below him; the hammer struck on a rock and a cartridge exploded. I had cautioned him several times on the trip never to carry more than five cartridges in the cylinder of his revolver, so that the hammer would always rest on an empty chamber, but he would not take my advice until this last accident. He got a forty-five-caliber bullet through the brim of his Stetson hat, which I think taught him a lesson that he will never forget. When the shot was fired the two men at camp jumped on their horses, which I suppose were saddled, and went to the hills. The man with the cattle did the same. We never got sight of any of them on account of being behind a bluff. We took charge of the camp and found that they had just been preparing for breakfast. A coffee pot filled with black coffee was simmering over a slow fire, and there was a frying pan with juicy antelope steak and a Dutch oven with biscuits, plenty of salt, onions and potatoes. We also found the mule that we had been trailing, picketed out near by. It was a large iron-gray, and a splendid animal. A pack saddle and equipment were also found.

First we rounded up the cattle and counted them. We found they were our cattle and corresponded to the number we had lost. Then we ate a hearty breakfast while one man was left on guard. After we finished our meal we packed everything that we thought we might need on the mule and turned him into the herd and pulled out for camp. When the foreman made a count of the entire herd, he found that we had all of our cattle. A party of us went down the Blue River leading the gray mule to see if the Indians had told us the truth about some white men living down there. First we found an adobe corral made out of sod, that would hold several hundred cattle or horses, and near by, some dugouts where we found some seven or eight villainous-looking white men, but none of them would claim the mule. As we had no evidence against them, we returned to camp, bringing the mule back with us. Afterwards we learned that this rendezvous on the Blue River was called 'Robbers' Roost,' and that this bunch of cutthroats made a business of stampeding horses or cattle on the northwestern trails, cutting off a bunch which they would butcher in the hills and then sell the beef at Fort Kearney, Nebraska. After we had driven our herd over to the Platte River, we met a scouting party of United States troops from Fort McPherson, a government post not far away. They told us that a band of Sioux Indians had massacred about eighty or one hundred Pawnee Indians the day before in Moran Canyon, a short distance above the Platte River. It appears that this party of Pawnee Indians had started out with their squaws and papooses to kill buffalo for winter meat and had camped in the Moran Canyon, which is a beautiful place, with plenty of high grass and water, but as the bluff was perpendicular on each side and very high, there was no way to get out of the canyon except by the way they went in, which was at the mouth.

A war party of Sioux Indians, which must have been

the same party that we ran into out in the hills, had probably crossed the trail of the Pawnee buffalo hunters, and located their camp in Moran Canyon. They rode up on a mesa, evidently in the night, picketing out some fifteen or twenty head of ponies near a thicket of wild cherry bushes in plain view of the canyon where the Pawnees were camped. They then stretched fresh buffalo hides over the ponies, with the horns on the hide, concealed themselves in the bushes and awaited developments. When the Indians are in camp they always arise early and the very first thing they do is to send some Indian up on the highest knoll about, to see what there is in sight. I presume in this case the first thing was what the Pawnee thought to be a bunch of buffalo across on the mesa near the wild cherry bushes; then reporting that buffalo were in sight, all the best men made a dash out of the canyon to circle the buffalo, leaving their old men and women and children in camp. When the Pawnee riders ran into the trap set for them, they were literally annihilated by their enemies in ambush. The Sioux then mounted their ponies and dashed into the Pawnee camp through the mouth of the canyon and massacred the entire bunch of Pawnees, including all their women and children.

The commanding officer at Fort McPherson, not far away, had in some way been notified of the massacre. He took a detachment of soldiers and went out and buried the mutilated bodies of the dead Pawnees. He found two little Indian boys about two or three years of age, that the Sioux Indians had overlooked, hidden

in the tall rye grass. The officer took the little fellows
home with him and I think adopted them.

The Pawnees had quite a drove of dogs with them, as
they usually do when going on a buffalo hunt. These
dogs all went to the hills, and I understand there were
wild dogs in that section for several years. This scouting party of soldiers took dinner with our outfit, then
went on down the Platte River, but before they left us
they relieved us of the gray mule, which they recognized as one of their pack animals which had been
stolen from Fort McPherson a short time before.

We finally got through to North Platte and delivered
our cattle. From the time we left Denton, Texas, until
we reached the Nebraska town, we had been on the
trail four months, and on a straight line. We had
traveled nearly a thousand miles over a country as wild
and virgin as it was in the days of Daniel Boone, or of
those other great explorers, Lewis and Clark. The only
spots where the country on this trail was settled were
the two railroad towns, Abilene and North Platte.

I have traveled much since I made this first boyhood
journey but none other has been so full of hardship
and peril. Yet the new scenes and experiences had
fascinated me with all their dangers.

North Platte at this time was a thriving little city.
The Union Pacific Railroad had a division point here.
This great transcontinental trunk line had just been
completed a few months before. This town, by the
way, was later the home of that noted scout and
plainsman, Honorable W. F. Cody (Buffalo Bill).

It was now well along in the month of September. The prairies had begun to take on the somber brown appearance that showed the approach of autumn, which in northwestern Nebraska means the approach of cold weather. I began to long for my home in the sunny South again; in fact, I was homesick. So in company with a young cowboy by the name of Crowell Walling, I started back by way of Abilene.

We packed one of our horses with sufficient supplies and took the trail by way of Moran Canyon, on towards Robbers' Roost, on Blue River. The second day out we camped in sight of three prairie schooners with the stove pipes sticking through the wagon sheets. We found the party was greatly alarmed and were afraid that they would be murdered by the hostile Indians that were infesting the country at that time. There was an old gentleman from Fort Laramie, Wyoming, with his wife and two daughters, and there were also a couple of young married women in the party. They were all on their way to Abilene, Kansas, which they expected to make their home. They were delighted to find traveling companions and incidentally guards, of course, and we were glad to help them out. We kept everybody supplied with buffalo and antelope meat. There was a good fiddler in the party, and after our work was done at night, we would spread out the tarpaulin and everybody would take part in an old-fashioned outdoor dance on the prairie. We had a delightful trip and regretted to have to part with our friends, especially the two young girls, when we reached Abilene.

When I arrived in Texas I remained at home all winter and in the spring of 1870 I again left home and went out west to Jack and Young counties in the Bellknap Mountains. About the time of my arrival in Jacksboro, the Kiowa and Comanche Indians were making trouble for the whites in northern Texas. They were constantly attacking the settlers, while at the same time they relied upon Uncle Sam for their bread and butter. They would draw their supplies from the United States agency at Fort Sill with a regularity that would have done credit to their fat, lazy, and peaceful brothers of later years. They would then make a beeline for their camp in the Wichita Mountains, where they would jerk their beef and give their ponies a rest. In the light of the next full moon they would start for the South, cross Red River into Texas, and commence their murderous raids. This Indian warfare continued along the border for many years. I never knew these Indians to capture a white man alive, unless he happened to be badly wounded and then they would torture him to death at once. The Kiowas and Comanches would sometimes adopt a white boy or girl into their tribe. One instance where they adopted a little girl was in the case of Cynthia Ann Parker, of Parker County, Texas, who was captured by the Comanches when she was a child. At the age of fifteen the Comanche chief married her. Quannah Parker, the noted chief who died at his home near Lawton, Oklahoma, a few years ago, was their son.

On the western side of the State the pioneers were

harassed by the most crafty and cruel Indians, the Apaches. The desert with its blinding and burning sands, which have been strewn with the bones of lost travelers, the desert which raises other unpleasant and uncompanionable things, such as cactus, centipedes, tarantulas, and rattlesnakes, also produced the Apache. He made a fit companion for these products of the arid and sun-baked wastes of the Southwest. The fiendish crimes of this tribe, led by the great Geronimo, were the capsheaf of the Devil's handiwork.

In the southern part of the State, especially along the Rio Grande, roamed the Mexican Greasers. Their unfriendly feeling for the American dated from the fall of the Alamo. Their hatred of the Texan was only equaled by the fear and respect in which they held their Gringo brother. The Mexicans were then looked upon with contempt and not feared except for their treachery.

Nearly every one carried guns in those days and many citizens acting individually or as possemen rendered valuable service on the side of law and order. The cowboy, like the Minute Man of the Revolution, was ready to act on the instant. It was from this immense array of cowboys that was developed one of the grandest and bravest organizations of officers that ever patrolled the plains, the Texas Rangers. A broncho-buster, an expert user of the rope, and a dead shot with the Winchester were his general qualifications, but more than this, he loved justice, right, and fair play, and was fighting for his loved ones and his home. The

Indian and the outlaw dreaded the Ranger more than the troops, most of whom were colored, that garrisoned the Southwest posts.

In the spring of 1871, one hundred and fifty Comanches and Kiowas from Fort Sill, under the leadership of the three chiefs, Satanta, Satank, and Big Tree, made a raid down into Jack County, Texas, and captured Warren's wagon train of freighters who were hauling supplies to Fort Griffin. This surprise on the government teamsters happened on Salt Creek Prairie, ten miles west of Jacksboro. After a desperate fight, lasting several hours, the Indians, by overwhelming numbers, killed seven teamsters besides scalping and mutilating them, and also captured the wagon train.

Along with the party was a cowboy who was badly wounded in this fight. The Indians chained him to a wagon wheel, then burned him with all the wagons. Some of the teamsters escaped by getting into buffalo wallows and remaining under cover until night. After the Indians had killed all the white men they could find, they drove the government mules back to the reservation at Fort Sill.

The next day after the massacre took place, General Sherman, Commanding General of the United States Army, who at that time was on a tour of inspection of posts along the border, passed over the spot where the massacre took place. When he arrived at Fort Sill he found the same band of Indians drawing rations and exhibiting fresh scalps of the freighters. He immediately ordered the commanding officer at Fort Sill to

arrest the three chiefs and deliver them to the civil
authorities at Jacksboro to be prosecuted for murder.
The Indians were arrested and placed in an army
wagon and with an escort of mounted troops on each
side started for Texas. Just after getting out of the
limits of the post, the old chief Satank, huddled down
in the wagon bed, pulled his blankets over his head and,
with his teeth, literally tore the flesh from his hands
until he was able to slip off one of the handcuffs. He
then grasped a buffalo skinning knife, which he had
concealed, and with the right hand plunged the knife
into the back of the teamster who was driving. The
soldiers riddled Satank with bullets.

Satanta and Big Tree were taken through in safety
to Jacksboro and turned over to the custody of Sheriff
Lee Crutchfield. Never have I seen people more in-
furiated than were the settlers of that community.
The Indians were moved for safe-keeping to Fort
Richardson, a government post about half a mile from
Jacksboro.

When court convened I was selected by the sheriff
and one of the guards to take the prisoners to and from
court during the trial, which lasted more than a week.
This case was prosecuted by Sam. T. Lanham, who
was afterwards Governor of Texas. He made an im-
passioned and eloquent address, one of the greatest
ever delivered in the prosecution of criminals. Its
literary merits have been recognized and it has been
given a place in many collections of our choicest
literature.

The Indians were convicted of murder in the first degree and sentenced to be hanged, but were pardoned by Governor Davis, and taken to Huntsville, Texas, where Satanta committed suicide after being punished for his refusal to work. Big Tree was paroled and went back to his tribe, but was returned to prison after he had started to make trouble again. He was pardoned the second time and now lives near Mount Scott, in the Wichita Mountains in Oklahoma.[1]

The trial and conviction of these Indians put an end to their depredations in Texas and southern Indian Territory. In a few years the frontier began to settle rapidly. A different class of people came to the West. There being no further danger from Indians, the tenderfeet drifted into the country and began to kill buffaloes for their hides; but when the buffalo was gone, some of them began stealing cattle and horses. This brought us a new period of outlawry which lasted well into the seventies. The Texas Rangers were again ordered out, this time to fight the white outlaw, instead of the Indian. During the next few years it was a never-ceasing conflict with horse thieves and bank robbers. There was one general name that would apply to nearly all of them, murderers. They were a wild, desperate bunch, and the blood of many a good officer was poured out before they were conquered. However, the Rangers slowly rounded up the outlaws and those who were not killed or sent to the penitentiary left to ply their trade in some other State.

[1] Big Tree died in November, 1929. (Editor.)

By the year 1878, Texas was comparatively quiet, too quiet in fact to suit me, so I decided to try the Northwest territory once more. I had had a desire to return to that country ever since I had gone north with Burk Burnett in sixty-nine.

CHAPTER II

INDIANS AND CATTLE THIEVES

IN the early summer of 1878, I started in charge of an outfit that was driving twenty-five hundred head of cattle from north Texas to Ogallala, Nebraska. This town is on the Union Pacific, about seventy-five miles west of North Platte.

About the same time that we started with these cattle, the Cheyenne Indians broke away from Fort Reno, Indian Territory, where they were being held as prisoners. After killing a number of white settlers in a swift raid across western Kansas and Nebraska, they crossed our path at Julesberg, Colorado. We were holding our cattle near a big pond called the Julesberg Water Hole. They were bedded for the night and were all lying down peaceful and quiet. After midnight a pungent odor caused by burning buffalo hair and skins was wafted to us by a stiff northern breeze. This was an old trick of the Plains Indians, as the smell of burnt hair will stampede cattle when nothing else will. We knew the Indians were upon us. After a few moments of sniffing, the terrified cattle rose all in an instant. We got in our saddles as quickly as possible and turned the leaders gradually until we had them running in a circle, and after a time they came to a stop. The Indians, however, got fifty of our best horses. The Cheyennes continued on to the northward, but were intercepted near Fort Robinson, Nebraska, where they surrendered to United States troops and were immediately placed in a stockade.

In a few days the entire band made a dash for liberty. Quite a number of them were killed by the soldiers and the remainder escaped. Among those who got away were two chiefs, Dull Knife and Two Moons, who were finally rounded up by General Miles in Montana near Fort Keough and placed on a small reservation on Rosebud Creek.

Soon after I delivered my herd at Ogallala, I accepted a position with the Wyoming Stock Raisers' Association as field inspector, with headquarters at Cheyenne. My duties were to take charge of the criminal work on the range, protect the interests of members of the Association, recover stolen property, and furnish evidence against stock thieves. I was sent to the Yellowstone River country in Montana, with headquarters at Miles City.

Tom Irvin, sheriff of Custer County, Montana, at this time and for many years after, gave me a commission as a regular deputy. W. D. Smith, an inspector for the Montana Stock Association, was assigned to work with me. The range which we covered extended from Miles City to Coulson, now Billings, Montana, and included the Yellowstone country and Crow Indian Reservation.

My first trip out was to the Little Big Horn River and Wolf Creek Mountains, where I went to investigate a report that the Crow Indians were killing some of our cattle and selling the beef for elk meat.

The first thing I did when I reached that country was to take advantage of the opportunity to look over the battleground where General Custer and two hundred and seventy-eight men were killed two years before. History calls this the 'Custer Massacre,' but according to the Indian custom I would call it a fair fight. Custer made the first attack on the Indians and after that they had to fight and they certainly did fight to a finish.

Of course they outnumbered Custer more than ten to one, but he started the fight and took his chances. No one knew better than General Custer that a Sioux on the warpath never takes an enemy prisoner. He was also informed that the Sioux and Cheyenne were well equipped for battle and knew as well how to fight in the hills as he did. He must have depended on Major Reno with his four hundred men, two miles away, to come to his support. No one will ever know what this gallant soldier and experienced Indian fighter had in his mind when he made this seemingly reckless attack.

Most of the details of this fight are matters of history with which nearly every one is familiar, but going over the battleground as I did, so soon after, I will take the liberty of describing this fight as I reconstructed it in my own imagination from the impressions that I received from viewing the battlefield and its surroundings. The Indians were encamped in a large valley on the opposite side of the Little Big Horn River from which Custer made the attack. Custer's last camp before the fight was on the Rosebud, fifteen miles to the east. He had made a cut-off by marching his command through the hills and bad lands, and attacked the main Indian camp on the river with the stream between him and them. The river here is narrow and very swift.

Two years later, as I looked over the battleground, I noticed the stakes that were driven up to mark the spot where each soldier fell. The bodies had all been removed, with the exception of that of Lieutenant Crittenden, who commanded a troop of the Seventh Cavalry during the fight. It was said that his father in Kentucky remarked that his gallant son died as a soldier should, and that he preferred to leave the remains of his son on the battlefield where he fell.

Any one who understands anything about Indian warfare, after looking the ground over, could plainly see why Custer and his men were killed. The stakes were driven up here, there, and everywhere, over about ten acres of ground, and, with one exception, showed no formation whatever. It showed that the officers must have lost control of their men. The exception was in the case of Lieutenant Crittenden's company. The stakes that marked his company's position were straight as an arrow. He was stationed to the southeast of where Custer fell. It was apparent that these men must have all died on the firing line with their commander at the head of the column. Considering the great number of the savage enemy and their crowded formation as they came on, eager to kill and scalp the doomed soldiers, no doubt many more Indians were

killed than were their white victims. It was probably
at the end of this one-sided struggle similar to the cases
of Colonel Bowie and Davy Crockett at the Alamo,
whose bodies were found beneath several of their
Mexican assailants, that they had killed in the final
death struggle.

General Custer fell on the point of a range or backbone, where a monument has since been placed in the
highest and most conspicuous point on the field. All
of his staff officers, several of whom were his relatives,
about fifteen Indian scouts, and more than a score of
horses were killed around him. The bones of the horses
were all in sight. Where Colonel Keough fell I counted
fifteen stakes driven up around him. They had evidently been shot down by one volley of fire, from a
bunch of wild cherry bushes about fifteen yards away.

When Custer first attacked the Indians on the banks
of the Little Big Horn River, the Indians must have
put up such a fierce fight that he could not cross the
stream, but was obliged to fall back into the Bad Lands
for protection. The Indians, evidently expecting this
move, had crossed the river in large numbers, two
hundred yards below, at the mouth of a large ravine.
This canyon headed back up in the hills where the last
stand was made. Its walls were so high that the Indians could keep well under cover until they had plenty
of time to select their positions. I think they did this
and in so doing cut off and completely surrounded
Custer's command. He found himself in a trap after
he retreated from the river back to the Bad Lands, from

which he could not escape. One lieutenant must have broken through the lines, as his dead body was found two miles away, with that of his horse. The only survivor of this battle was a Crow Indian named Curly. He was serving as a scout at this time. He could tell me nothing definite about the conflict except to say, 'Heap big fight! Indians heap shoot soldiers like h—l all time from bush.'

After finishing our observations, we left the hills and went down to a camp and arrested two Crow Indians for stealing cattle. We took them to Miles City and placed them in jail. The sheriff was having a scaffold erected in the jail yard at the time we put the Indians in jail. One of the prisoners had told the Indians the scaffold was being built for them. That night the Indians took pieces of buckskin thong from their moccasins and after wetting them thoroughly tied them tight around their necks. The next morning the jailer found them both dead. When the buckskin had dried up it had tightened around their throats and choked them to death.

At that time the terminus of the Northern Pacific Railroad was at Miles City and the only means of travel west of there was by saddle horse or stagecoach. This railroad company had furnished free transportation from the East to all laborers who wanted to go West. The loose criminal element in New York, Chicago, and other cities took advantage of this opportunity to leave the Eastern States. The result was that the country west of Miles City, Montana, was

soon overrun with the most desperate gang of cut-
throats that ever went unhung. The cattle thieves
and the stage robbers along the Yellowstone were bad
enough, but when this bunch of city thugs was turned
loose the law-abiding citizens were surrounded by un-
bearable conditions.

Stolen cattle were driven into railroad camps and
sold to contractors at half their value. Horses were
stolen in broad daylight. It was not an unusual sight
to see floating down the river the body of some railroad
laborer, with his throat cut or a bullet hole through him,
who had been robbed and murdered after receiving his
week's pay. Sheriff Irvin and his deputies were working day and night. Many criminals were convicted
and sentenced to the penitentiary at Deer Lodge,
Montana. Quite a number broke jail and escaped. I
remember at one time we had seventy-five prisoners
in the old stockade at Miles City, most of them desperate men. The officers were brave and determined,
and did their duty, but there were not enough of them.
The actual residents in Montana then took a hand in
the game. The miners and ranchmen organized vigilance committees in many different localities. The
thieves would be given fair warning to leave the country or take their medicine, but they never received a
second warning. If the first warning was not obeyed,
you would probably find several dead bodies hanging
to telegraph poles. The vigilantes soon ran the crooks
out of the towns. Then Granville Stuart, president
of the Montana Stock Association, at the head of fifty

cowboys, commenced a war of extermination against
the criminals on the range, along the Yellowstone and
Musselshell, and the Missouri rivers. Early Montana
history has recorded what Granville Stuart and his
cowboys did that made it possible for an honest man to
live in Montana and enjoy the fruits of his labor. The
criminals who were fortunate enough to get out of
Montana alive all came south into Wyoming and
Idaho. They knew if they went north and crossed the
Missouri River they would be in Canada and have the
Northwest Mounted Police to deal with, which was not
much encouragement to a horse thief.

I moved from Miles City in 1880 and settled at
Buffalo, in Johnson County, Wyoming, but I was still
in the employ of the Wyoming Stock Association. I
secured four hundred and eighty acres of land twelve
miles southwest of Buffalo at the foot of the Big Horn
Mountains and commenced farming and stock raising.
At that time Johnson County, Wyoming, covered an
immense area of land. The eastern boundary was
South Dakota, the northern line was Montana, and the
southern line was Albany County on the North Platte
River. West of Buffalo it had taken in all of the Big
Horn and Wind River Mountains out to the line of
Idaho. The mountains were full of big game, elk, bear,
and mountain sheep and black-tailed deer; while the
valleys were covered with antelope and some buffalo.
It was the best rendezvous for outlaws that I have ever
seen, and they were there, plenty of them.

I was elected sheriff of Johnson County in 1882. At

SHERIFF FRANK M. CANTON OF JOHNSON COUNTY, WYOMING

that time our nearest railroad point was Rock Creek, Wyoming, two hundred and fifty miles south of Buffalo on the Union Pacific Railroad. This trip was made over a stage line. Later on, when the Northern Pacific Railroad was completed, we traveled to Custer Station, Montana, one hundred and fifty miles north of Buffalo. We had no penitentiary at that time and the territorial authorities made a contract with the State of Illinois to keep our convicts at Joliet. I appointed John McDermott my undersheriff, to take charge of the office work. He was an excellent clerical man and a brave and loyal officer. I selected eighteen picked men for field deputies, who knew the country and were especially fitted for such work. I had but little time to stay in my office for the next two years, for I was in charge of the field work myself, and in the saddle most of the time. District court convened at Buffalo once a year. We always had a large bunch of convicts after court to take over the long trip by stagecoach to the railroad, then to Joliet. It would sometimes take two stagecoaches for the prisoners and guards.

In 1885 I married Annie Wilkerson, daughter of W. H. Wilkerson, who moved out from Illinois with his family and settled near the little town of Big Horn, Wyoming. My wife liked the country and we were very happy in our new home.

During those days the worst criminals we had to deal with were the stage robbers, or road agents, as they were called in that country. The Wells Fargo treasure was carried by stagecoach through the mountains from

Rock Creek, Wyoming, to Custer Station, Montana —
a distance of four hundred and fifty miles. While the
United States Government had offered a standing reward of one thousand dollars for the arrest and conviction of each stage robber, hardly a week passed but
that the stage was robbed somewhere along the line,
and the driver generally shot down from ambush.
Several United States paymasters were robbed and
large amounts taken, until finally Big-Nosed George,
leader of the gang, was shot down and killed and three
of his men captured and sentenced for life. Shortly
after the death of Big-Nosed George I captured the
notorious stage robber, Bill Brown, and his partner on
Pinney Creek, north of Buffalo. These two outlaws
were both tried in federal court in Cheyenne, Wyoming, and sentenced for life. T. Jeff Carr, one of the best-
known officers in that part of the country, helped me
get the evidence to convict these two men. This put
a damper on stage robbing in the northwest.

The Black Hills gold excitement had brought many
people into South Dakota. The mines were paying
well, and this made a good market for work horses and
mules. The country in Idaho, Utah, Oregon, and
Nevada was overstocked with ranch horses and no
market for them whatever. There was a notorious
outlaw who had a rendezvous with his gang in Jackson's Hole, Idaho, and in the Teton Mountains. He
was called Teton Jackson. This man had run a pack
train for General Crook during the Sioux war. He was
placed in the guard house for stealing government

mules. He killed two soldiers and escaped to the Teton
Mountains. He was a Mormon and was a member of
a gang of Mormon outlaws whom they called Destroy-
ing Angels. John D. Lee, who was executed for the
Mountain Meadows massacre, was his uncle. Jackson
was a most dangerous and vicious character. He had
killed several Deputy United States Marshals in Utah
and Idaho, who had followed him into the mountains.
The Territory of Utah had offered three thousand five
hundred dollars reward for his capture, dead or alive,
but as he could always get assistance from one of the
Mormons in any of their settlements along the borders
of Idaho and Utah, it was almost impossible to get an
even break with him. He had about a dozen hard men
with him. When he found that they could sell horses
in the Black Hills for a good price, they began stealing
horses from the rangers in the adjoining territories.
The system this band adopted was to steal ten or
fifteen head from each herd on the range scattered over
a large area of country, and drive them into Jackson's
Hole, which was a basin of country covering several
square miles, and was almost completely walled in by
mountains. Twenty-five years ago this was the most-
talked-of outlaw rendezvous in the world. The owners
would probably not miss their stock for months, and
even then would think the little bunch had strayed off.

When the thieves had secured eight hundred or one
thousand head, they would then doctor the brands and
as soon as the new brands healed over they would put
the herd on the trail and drive them over through

Johnson County, Wyoming, to Deadwood and other mining towns in the Black Hills where they would find a good market for them. This systematic stealing continued for several years. One day I received a telegram from Billy Hosford, an officer whom I knew at Blackfoot, Idaho, saying that Teton Jackson had recently stolen about fifty head of fine horses from two ranchmen by the names of High and Stout, and that he was seen by two Snake Indians heading toward the Big Horn Basin.

There was an old trapper and hunter by the name of Lucas, who had a cabin at the mouth of Paint Rock Creek Canyon in the Basin, whom I suspected of being in league with this band of horse thieves. His cabin was forty miles from Buffalo over the Big Horn Mountains. I selected Chris Gross and Ed Loyd, two of my best deputies, and left Buffalo about dark, and by hard riding through pine timber and windfalls, reached the cabin about two hours before daylight. We tied our horses to some trees and got positions in good shooting distance of the cabin, which had only one door and one window. Of course, we did not know that Teton was there and only suspected that he was in the cabin. But I did not intend to take any more chances than I would have done had I been sure that he was there. Just before daybreak a candle was lighted in the cabin and in a few minutes sparks began to come out of the chimney. We then approached nearer the cabin. I gave my Winchester to Gross and Loyd and gave orders for them to watch the window and door and stop any one who might try to escape. I then drew my six-shooter and stepped quietly into the cabin. I recognized Teton Jackson instantly by the description I had of him. He was squatted down in front of the fireplace trying to light his pipe with a splinter. He was only half dressed and had not yet buckled on his six-shooter, although it was lying within his reach with a belt full of cartridges. I covered him at once with my revolver, and ordered him to throw up his hands, and at the same time called for my deputies to come in and handcuff him. Lucas was slicing up venison for breakfast. There were two other men in a bunk in the cabin, whom I had supposed were with Teton, but when we had them all lined up I found that these two men were hunters, who were traveling about skinning wolves for their pelts. After we had breakfast I sent Lucas out with my two deputies and told him that if he did not round up and bring in every horse that Teton had driven into the canyon I would arrest him too and take him to Buffalo.

After they left I was in the cabin alone with Teton. He was not a pleasant companion. I have never seen a man of his description before or since. He was about forty-five, over six feet in height, weight a hundred and ninety, stubby beard, raw-boned, coarse features, flaming red hair, red face, and eyes as black as a snake's. He told me that he had two men to help him to drive the bunch himself and had sent his two men back to Jackson's Hole. I had taken a seat about six feet from him with my revolver in my hand. He began to complain that the handcuffs were so tight that the blood could not circulate and that he was in great pain, and that if I would take them off he would keep quiet and promise not to hurt me. I told him that I was not the least bit uneasy about his hurting me, and that I had no objection to granting his request, but that he was the one that was taking all the chances, for if he made the slightest move I would kill him. He said he understood the situation. I then threw the keys over to him, and he unlocked the handcuffs and pitched the keys and cuffs back to me.

After he had removed the cuffs he began rubbing his wrists and said that I would never take him to Buffalo and that he wanted to serve notice on me right there and then that he was a better man than I was, even without a six-shooter. He began to talk very abusive. I told him that I would take him to Buffalo and that he was worth as much to me dead as alive. I told him I would prefer to take his dead body as it would be less trouble to handle than a live one. I then threw the open handcuffs on the floor at his feet and told him that if he did not snap them on his wrists in ten seconds, he could take his medicine. I think he put them on in less time than I had given him.

My deputies returned in about an hour with the stolen horses, which proved to be the property of High and Stout. We put Teton on one of the horses, tied his feet together under the horse's body, and landed him in jail in Buffalo that night.

The only trouble we had was in crossing a little

meadow on top of the mountains. The meadow was not more than fifty yards across, but the sod was underlaid with thin mud, six to eight feet deep. It would bear up a horse, crossing singly, but the bunch being ahead cut the turf enough so that my horse broke through. I jumped off and broke through the bog with one foot, so it threw me down and my horse struggled and floundered around until he got on the turf again before I got to my feet. Teton was watching me while I was having this trouble and when my horse got on his feet again, he trotted ahead leaving me afoot, and went right up by the side of Jackson. My Winchester was in the scabbard, and Teton saw his opportunity at once and was just reaching down for it when I called to the deputies to look out. Ed Loyd drew his six-shooter just in time to make the desperate outlaw let the gun alone.

As I got on my horse again, Teton said, 'If I could have got that gun I would have settled with you anyway.'

It was a close call, but 'an inch of a miss is as good as a mile.'

Billy Hosford, officer from Idaho, came over after the prisoner and took him to Blackfoot, where he was sentenced for a long term for horse stealing. They had several murder cases against him, but it would have taken some time to secure the evidence, and the officers were afraid to keep him in jail at Blackfoot for fear that his gang would rescue him. He was taken to Boise City and placed in the penitentiary. After he had been there about a month, I received a letter from him to the effect that I had always treated him well, that I was doing my duty in capturing him, that he, Teton, had nothing against me, and in fact would go out of his way to do me a favor. The outlaw continued that the State of Idaho did not furnish tobacco to prisoners, that he had no money to buy it with, and concluded by begging me to send him a dollar or two so he could get some. I wrote him a short note, and enclosed him a twenty-dollar bill. A short time after that — as I remember it, not more than two or three months — Teton broke out of the prison — dug under the wall, I believe — and has never been heard of since. To show the gratitude of the man, and to show how twenty dollars had softened his heart, he left a note in his cell containing a list of the names of a dozen different men whom he was going to kill on sight, no matter where or when he met them. My name was the first one on the list. The reward offered by the Territory of Idaho was paid. I divided it equally with my two deputies.

Teton Jackson out of the way, the backbone of the band was broken. Red Anderson and Black Tom, two members of the band, were shot and killed near the Yellowstone Park. George Stevens, alias Big George, was shot and killed on the Big Horn Mountains by Chris Gross, who also captured Frank Lamb. The rest of the gang left the Teton Mountains and most of them were picked up by officers in adjoining territories and sent to the penitentiary. Up to this time we had convicted many horse thieves and had succeeded in breaking up one of the best organized gangs of stage robbers in the Northwest.

However, I knew that there were many hard characters still in the country who had managed to keep under cover, and at the same time were aiding the outlaws in every way possible. One of these was a man named Arapaho Brown, a white man who had formerly lived with the Arapaho Indians until he had done some dirty work, for which he was driven out of that tribe. He must have come to Johnson County in early days, for he was there when I first came to the country; living on a little ranch about ten miles northwest of Buffalo. He was a smooth talker, and one of the most powerful men physically in the country. He was vicious, cruel, and crafty and would 'double-cross' his grandmother if he had a chance. He had a great deal of influence with the criminal element in the country.

There had been more than one man who had mysteriously disappeared from his neighborhood, that Arapaho Brown had been suspected of having murdered, but no evidence could ever be procured. He always kept a few villainous-looking men about his place, but no one knew where they came from. One of these was a fellow named Bill Booth, who would come into town about every two weeks, buy tobacco and strychnine, and claim to be poisoning wolves for their pelts. An old German bachelor by the name of Jake Smearer lived in Red Hills, eight miles southeast of Buffalo, on a little hay ranch from which he made a living from hay cut off his meadow. This man Booth had been in the habit of coming into Jake's cabin at night to sleep and was seen there several times by a colored man who lived near by. One day it was reported to me that old Jake was missing and that his cabin door was locked. I began to investigate and found that he had not been to town for some time, but that he had contracted about a week before to sell his little ranch for five hundred dollars. I summoned a posse, and took them out to his cabin. We found the door locked and no one about the house. Everything seemed to be in place. There were a great many blood spots on the wall, but this was not strange, as Jake had been in the habit of shooting antelope for his meat and hanging the fresh meat up on the wall of his cabin, which was liable to leave blood stains. But the fact that his wagon was at the cabin and his team of horses gone looked suspicious to me. And as Bill Booth was also missing, and had not been seen in the country for several weeks, I was satisfied that there had been foul play. We searched the Red Hills in the vicinity of the cabin for two days, hunting for the dead body of Jake, but without success.

I then told a colored man who lived near that if he would find the body I would pay him one hundred dollars. In a few days he reported to me that he had found Jake's body. I summoned the coroner and went out with the colored man to a little canyon about two miles from Jake's cabin, where the body was found in the canyon covered up with small boulders. His skull had been crushed in several places with some blunt weapon. The murderer had tied a cord very tightly around his victim's neck to stop the flow of blood. He then wrapped the murdered man's coat around his head, tied a string around that, and then carried him out to the canyon where he concealed the body.

I traced Jake's two horses to Deadwood, two hundred miles east of Buffalo, and found that they had been sold to the proprietor of the Elephant Corral, a wagon yard in Deadwood, by a man who suited the description of Booth so well that there was not much chance for a mistake. Then I sent descriptive cards out to nearly every officer in the Northwest, offering five hundred dollars reward for Bill Booth. In a few weeks I received a wire from my old friend, W. D. Smith, stock inspector, to the effect that he had captured Booth at Stonesville, Montana.

I wired him to bring the prisoner up to Custer Station on the Yellowstone, and that I would meet him there at the end of the stage line.

During the stage trip from Custer Station to Buffalo, by using some strategy, I got a confession out of Booth relative to killing Jake, although he tried to justify himself by saying that he had a row with the old German and had to kill him in self-defense, and then he hid the body for fear that he would not get a fair trial. He did not know that I had found Jake's horses. After I had locked him up in jail some of Jake's old friends got a crowd together, and secured a rope with the intention of hanging the prisoner, but after I talked with them a few minutes they changed their minds.

Before the lawyers got hold of him, Booth made a
written statement to me, with his signature to it.

When court convened he was convicted of willful
murder and sentenced to hang. H. S. Elliott, one of
the brightest young lawyers in Wyoming, was appointed by the court to defend him. He got a stay of
execution for Booth, for ninety days. Booth was the
hardest man to keep in jail that I ever handled. From
the moment I first turned the keys on him up to the
day of his execution he never ceased to try to escape,
and came near doing it several times. I kept him
shackled in his cell all the time and never used the
patent shackles. The shackles, or leg irons, that I used
were made by Harry Hollaway, the best blacksmith in
the country. They were put on the prisoner by the
blacksmith himself, who would brad and rivet hard
and fast. The next morning the links of the chains between the ankles would be broken off, and the prisoner
loose, but of course inside the cell. I would then send
for the blacksmith who would look at the broken
shackles in amazement, then put another pair on him.
This happened several times until I was afraid to have
his cell door opened without a revolver in my hand.

One night I concealed myself in the jail corridor to
watch and see if I could find out how he 'pulled off'
this stunt. I soon saw him at work. He had his back
tight up against the steel cell, then commenced a cir-
cular motion with his right foot until he had the chain
badly twisted. He would then brace his back against
his cell and straighten his right leg out with such force

and strength that it would snap the links of the chain. He seemed to have superhuman strength in his legs. Then I had the blacksmith put a swivel in the chain of the next pair he made for him. This broke up his game, for of course the chain would turn with the swivel and would not twist. He then invented another plan. He would often ask me for writing pens and paper to write letters, although he never sent any letters out. The priest, whom I permitted to go into his cell and counsel with him, gave him a small brass statue representing the crucifixion of Christ. Booth had taken the writing pens that I had given him, and hammered them out flat with the little brass statue, given him by the priest, then he would fasten one very ingeniously to a spare-rib that he had saved from his dinner. He would then hold the pen over the flame of a candle until he had taken the temper from it and made it soft, and with another pen, which was hard and of the finest steel, he sawed small notches in the soft pen and made a fine saw. This he hardened in some way by using the sperm from the candle while the candle was hot. With this he sawed off the rivets from the shackle of one leg as smoothly as it could have been cut with a cold chisel. The irons then dropped off his ankle. He put the shackle back around his ankle so that it would look all right and tied it up with some strands of thread, but in such a way that the least jerk of his foot would set him free.

When I opened his cell door the next morning, he had a note in his hand which he said he wanted me to hand to the priest, and made a quick step towards me, but I instantly covered him with my revolver, and it was a good thing for me that I did, for when he stepped towards me the irons fell from his legs. I will never forget the look he gave me. I then chained him to his cell on the inside with a chain long enough for some exercise so that he would not suffer, and kept a death watch over him until the execution.

When he first asked me to allow a minister to come to his cell I sent for Reverend Sparrow, who in his young days had been an officer of the law. I told him I would like to know the prisoner's history if he could get it.

When he went into Booth's cell he said, 'Booth, you have sworn that you killed Jake Smearer in self-defense. If you told the truth you are an innocent man. If you did not tell the truth, you are guilty. Which must I pray for, a guilty man, or an innocent man?'

Booth said, 'Pray for a guilty man.'

He also told the minister that he was born in Tippecanoe, Ohio, and that he deserted his wife and child there, and that they followed him to the Indian Territory; that he murdered them both and buried them in the hills near the old Pawnee Agency, now Pawnee, Oklahoma. A few days later he sent for the Catholic priest who was with him at his execution.

CHAPTER III

SAMUEL AND BEAVER

In 1884 I was reëlected sheriff by a large majority. By this time Johnson County had become well stocked with ranch cattle and horses. None of the Indians in that county at that time were openly on the warpath, as they had all been placed on their different reservations. But they were very restless and it was not safe for a white man alone to meet them in the hills, when they were on a hunting trip. The Crow reservation was seventy-five miles north of Buffalo, Montana. The Arapahoes and Shoshones were at Fort Washakie, two hundred miles southwest. The Sioux and Cheyenne were east of us, and the Snakes were west over the Idaho line, but all these tribes hunted through the mountains in Johnson County. As the big game became scarce they began to kill cattle.

The Arapaho and Shoshone Indians had one reservation and agency in common, located on Wind River, in Frémont County, Wyoming, about one hundred and forty miles northwest from Rawlins, a town on the Union Pacific Railroad. Each tribe was different from the other in all its affairs of government, and lived on different parts of the reservation, but not being large tribes one agent sufficed for both. Washakie was head chief of the Shoshones, and after the tribe was placed on the reservation, he was always a firm, true friend of the whites.

He was a noted Indian throughout Wyoming, Colorado, and Utah, had great influence with his people, and prevented the young bucks from making many a raid on the white settlers.

In the Arapaho tribe Black Coal was the head chief and was so recognized by the United States Government. He was a great warrior in his younger days, but, like Washakie, after he consented to his tribe being placed upon the reservation, he was always a friend of the whites. I think he was one of the finest-looking Indians I have ever seen, close to six feet in height, with a splendid physique, and with a head and face that would attract attention in any gathering. He could speak no English but was very bright and intelligent, very determined and resolute, and at the same time a man with a great deal of good, hard sense. He died during the summer of 1901.

Notwithstanding Black Coal was head chief of all the Arapahoes, there was a faction in the tribe headed by an Indian named Sharp Nose that was always trying to make trouble. He was the opposite of Black Coal in every way — in character, in disposition, in intelligence, and in honor. Black Coal had a high sense of honor, and if he gave his word that he would do some certain thing, one could be sure that if it were in his power to accomplish it that thing would be done. Sharp Nose, on the contrary, never would do anything that he agreed to unless it was for his own interest. He was deceitful, cruel, with a face more like a wild-cat than a human being, and was a bitter enemy of

Washakie and Black Coal and always most bitter towards the whites. He had a following of nearly five hundred in his band and the village always camped by itself. The worst characters and the most turbulent spirits of the Arapaho tribe were under him, and while he had some good Indians in his band, as a whole they were a bad lot.

For years the hunting grounds for the Arapaho Indians had been north and east from the reservation in the Owl Creek Mountains, Big Horn Mountains, and on the heads of Powder River, while the Shoshones hunted north and west from the reservation in the Wind River Range and Shoshone Mountains. For several seasons parties from Sharp Nose's band had made a practice, when on their hunting trips in the fall of each year, of killing cattle belonging to the rangemen whose ranches were in the Big Horn Basin, and also those who lived on the east side of the Big Horn Mountains on the heads of the Powder River. The '76, E K, W, C Y, and the Shield brands were the most frequent sufferers, and the Wyoming Stock Association had made every effort to catch the Indians in the act with proof enough for conviction, but with no success. The inspectors for the Association, the sheriffs of the different counties, and the cowboys of all the interested ranches were continually on the watch. They were constantly finding where animals had been killed, but only the feet and heads were left. The ears had been cut off close to the head and burned to get rid of any testimony in the way of ear marks, and the hides had either been burned or made into ropes to get rid of the brands.

Frequently the boys would come across camps of Indians with beef in their possession, cut in strips and either spread on scaffolds or hung on ropes to dry and cure in the sun for winter use. When questioned the Indians claimed that it was elk meat, and although the boys knew better, there was no proof to the contrary that any court could accept. So it went on from one year to another, the Indians getting bolder all the time and killing cattle more frequently, but never relaxing in their cunning, or in their vigilance not to be surprised by white men while they were killing beef.

I had been trying for a long time to get a case against the Indians that would 'hold water,' feeling sure that one conviction of an Indian to even a short term in the penitentiary would put a stop to all depredations on the ranchmen. Going into a camp or village of Indians to arrest one for stealing was something that up to that time had rarely been attempted by any but army officers backed up by a company of soldiers, and even they were not hankering for the job.

Undersheriff John McDermott, deputy Chris Gross, and myself worked for a long time trying to catch some Indians red-handed, but always unsuccessfully. Then I had an inspiration in the shape of two hunters named George McClennan and Bill Glass. The Territory of Wyoming had offered a standing reward of two hundred and fifty dollars for evidence leading to the arrest and conviction of horse and cattle thieves. McClennan and Glass were old hunters and trappers, lived in the Big Horn Mountains, and made their living by killing

bear for the oil and hides, and trapping beaver. I sent
for them, explained the condition of things and offered
them the Territorial reward if they would bring me the
necessary evidence for the conviction of these Indians.
They agreed to be on the lookout and went back to the
mountains.

It was only four or five weeks after that when the
hunters again appeared in Buffalo late one afternoon
leading a pinto pony, on which was an Indian saddle
packed with a beef hide. They reported to me that the
day before on the west slope of the mountains, about
twenty-five miles from Buffalo, they were following a
bear trail. They had just crossed a little spring branch,
one of the heads of Spring Creek which runs into No
Wood Creek in the basin, and just as they came up out
of the little canyon of the creek they ran onto two
young Indians in the act of skinning a cow which they
had evidently just shot. The Indians were not more
than a hundred yards away, but they saw McClennan
and Glass come out of the canyon. They had two ponies, one a black, which was standing close to them, the
other a pinto which was tied to a sage brush about fifty
feet away. Both Indians picked up their rifles, jumped
on the black pony, and made their escape down the
mountain before the hunters could make any effort to
stop them. All that McClennan and Glass could swear
to about the Indians was that both were young and
that one in particular was very fine-looking. They
took possession of the pony, finished skinning the cow,
which belonged to the C Y herd, cut off the ears, took

about seventy-five pounds of the best part of the meat, all they could conveniently carry, rolled the ears and meat in the hide, packed it on the pony, and started for Buffalo.

They also found lying on the ground close by the cow an old Stetson hat, cowboy style, which at one time had been nearly white, and an Indian medicine bag, which they took with them. When I looked the outfit over I found at once that my trouble had only just begun. Heretofore, I had had the Indians and beef, but no brand or ear marks as proof of ownership, while I now had all the proof I needed at that time, but the Indians were yet to be found and lodged in jail at Buffalo. I knew, too, that hunting for some particular Indian in the mountains was like hunting for the proverbial needle in the haystack. It was quite the proper thing for a cowboy to print with indelible ink on the inside of the brim of the light-colored Stetson hats they all wore all the brands he represented. I knew from the style and shape of the medicine bag that these two Indians were Arapahoes, and in examining the hat I soon found that some name had been written on the brim. It had from exposure to the weather become so dim that only after holding it under a magnifying glass was I able to decipher the word 'Samuel.' This was not much of a clue, as the hat might have belonged to some cowboy by that name. However, the hat, pony, saddle, and medicine bag were all I had to work from, so I began making my plans at once with them as a starter.

First, I wrote to the secretary of the Wyoming Stock Association at Cheyenne, Thomas Sturgis, telling him of all the happenings up to that time and asking him to have the proper authorities at Washington instruct the Indian agent at Fort Washakie to turn the two Indians over to me in case I had to go as far as the reservation for them, knowing that there had never been an Indian arrested and taken off that reservation, and that we would never get away alive if we undertook it without the sanction of the agent. I thought, however, that the Indians belonged to some small hunting party who were camped in the basin near the mouth of Spring Creek, and that it was likely they had gone down there after leaving the beef and that we would find them within a few miles of that place.

The commissary department, together with plenty of ammunition, was attended to that night, and the next morning about sunrise we left Buffalo for the mountains. The party consisted of myself, deputy Chris Gross, and the two hunters, McClennan and Glass, four in all. We had good saddle horses and took two pack horses besides the pinto pony.

It was two hundred long weary miles to the agency. The first night we camped on the little creek where the cow was killed, and in the morning we took up the trail of the pony on which the two Indians had made their escape. The trail ran straight to No Wood Creek, about ten miles, and here we found signs of quite a hunting party having been camped. As nearly as we could tell from the scaffolds for drying meat and from signs of tepees, the party must have consisted of nearly one hundred. Evidently when the two Indians came into camp and told their story of having been surprised while skinning the C Y cow, the whole party became frightened and started at once for the reservation. The trail looked to be two days old, but was big and plain, and I realized that I had to go to the agency for my Indians. I also recalled that Black Coal and his village were camped at the forks of Wind River and that from there to Fort Washakie up Little Wind River was twenty-five miles, with Indian camps scattered along for the whole distance. To carry out my plans and to save the horses all we could, we used up the rest of that day and the next three days getting to the Forks, and went into camp just at dark, two miles below Black Coal's village.

After getting supper and resting our horses for a few hours, I told my men that I wanted two of them and both pack horses to go with me to the agency that night, that the fourth man was to keep his saddle horse and the pinto pony and stay there in the camp until morning; then to pack some steel traps which the hunters had with them on the pinto pony, tie the white hat and the medicine bag on the pony where they could be seen plainly, and come to the agency. I hoped that some Indian would claim either the pony, hat, or medicine bag, and knowing the superstition of Indians about the latter, I felt sure that if the owner happened to see it he would take great chances in order to get possession of it again. I picked Bill Glass

for this work, principally because he was an expert in
talking the 'sign language.' I told Glass that if an
Indian claimed the pony or either of the articles to
give them up, but to get his name if possible, at any
rate to get such a mind photograph of the Indian that
he would surely know him if he ever saw him again.
The reason that I wanted only one man with the pony
was that many of the Indians knew me by sight and
knew that I was sheriff of the county, so I thought
if the party went together that the Indians would at
once become suspicious and even if the owner saw the
pony he would not dare claim him. The pony was one
of their best, what was known as a war pony, and the
fact of a lone white man leading him past the Indian
camps gave enough of the spice of danger to the trip
to make it a pleasure to Glass.

All this planning, however, did no good, as Glass
made the ride, and talked with a number of Indians, but
none of them would even look at the pony. We reached
the agency about daylight and went into camp near
by on the river. After getting breakfast we went to
the office of the Indian agent and asked to see the
record book, a book kept by the agent in which he
records the Indian name of every member of the tribe,
together with their names translated into English.
After searching for quite a while I found the name
Samuel. Then I questioned the clerk and learned that
he was a young Arapaho belonging to Sharp Nose's
band. The clerk said, 'He is a very fine-looking Indian,
good-hearted, has plenty of nerve, and is really too fine

to be under such an old scoundrel as Sharp Nose.' He
had within the last month married a young squaw
named Mollie, belonging to Black Coal's band. Mollie
was for years in the Indian school at Carlisle. She
spoke good English, wrote a beautiful hand, and was
noted for being the handsomest squaw in the Arapaho
tribe.

Just then the agent himself came in and I explained
to him my business, showing my warrants for the arrest of the two Indians, and asked the agent to turn
them over to me. The agent, when the honesty and
good behavior of his wards was called in question, was
like all other Indian agents whom I have ever known.
He got on his dignity at once, and declared that none
of his Indians ever did any wrong.

He said, 'Can you identify these two Indians?'

I said, 'Yes, I have two men with me who can
positively identify them.'

This was a great bluff on my part, for I had no proof
yet that I was sure of. The agent then said, 'If that
is so, you go and bring in your Indians and if you can
convince me that they are the right ones, you can take
them, but,' he went on to say, 'if I had not received
telegraphic instructions from Washington to turn
them over to you, I would never allow you to take
them.'

Then I tried to get the agent to ask Captain X, who
was in command of Fort Washakie, the Government
post for the reservation which was a mile away, to send
a reliable guard with me to the village of Sharp Nose,

but the agent refused. The only help he would give
was to permit his clerk to go with me and show us
where Sharp Nose was camped, but he gave his clerk
strict orders not to point out Samuel or to help in any
way. As I wanted a report from Glass before making
any further move, I decided not to start until dark, and
during the day I cultivated the acquaintance of the
clerk, who proved to be a right good fellow.

As soon as it was dark our party, including the clerk,
started back down Little Wind River to find Samuel.
The moon was past the full and rose about nine o'clock,
so that it was quite light from that time on. Shortly
after, we discovered that an Indian had followed us
from the agency, and that he was trying to get ahead of
us in the canyon. We rounded him up quickly, tying his
feet together under the horse which we led, to prevent
the Indian from giving any alarm. About midnight
we reached the camp of Sharp Nose, which was located
on a little flat in the edge of the timber bordering the
river. I dismounted about one hundred yards away
and left McClennan to hold the horses and to see that
the Indian did not escape or make any noise. In this
bend of the river Sharp Nose had about forty lodges,
and while the clerk knew very nearly where Samuel's
tepee was, he could not at night locate the exact one.
Everything was quiet as a graveyard, not even a dog
barking, which seemed singular in an Indian camp.
While working towards the first tepee each gathered a
handful of white sage, which was plentiful and as dry
as tinder. On reaching the tepee I touched a match to

a bunch of it, lifted the flap, and walked in among the sleeping Indians. The Indians all started up, of course, but the strong light which blinded them showed me that the man I wanted was not in that tepee. We hurried out and into the next one and so on until we had entered four with no success. The Indians from the tepees that we had entered had stampeded and taken to the brush, but so far had not made noise enough to awaken the rest of the camp.

The fifth tepee was the largest one in the camp and the clerk whispered as we entered that it was the lodge of Sharp Nose. I found eight Indians in this lodge just rousing from sleep, two of them on one side by themselves, under a fine buffalo robe. I pulled the robe off and uncovered a young squaw and a young buck that answered the description of Samuel so well that I took hold of him and told him to get up on his feet.

The squaw spoke at once in good English and said, 'You are not going to take Sam, are you?'

I said, 'Yes, I must take him with me. Your name is Mollie, isn't it?'

She answered, 'Yes.'

By that time I had handcuffs on Samuel and we had started out of the lodge, Gross and I holding on to him while we made a run for our horses.

The camp by that time was in an uproar. It was bedlam turned loose, Indians running in every direction catching and saddling horses, dogs howling and barking, squaws chanting war songs, and with war whoops mingled with the rest of the noise. I had taken the precaution to set saddles back on the horses and tighten the cinches before leaving them, and I now put Samuel on the pinto pony, which we had brought along for that purpose, tied his feet together under the horse, turned loose the Indian that we had captured on our way down, and started on a fast ride for Fort Washakie, twenty miles away. We got away without having to fire a shot. While the Indians were saddling their horses and getting ready to pursue, I secured enough of a start so that I was in the Fort ahead of them.

The officer of the guard met us as we rode into the post and went with me to the house of Captain X, whom we awakened.

I told him what I had done, and said, 'What assistance can you give me in case Sharp Nose tries to take Samuel away from me?'

The captain's reply was the first word of encouragement I had received since I started on the trip.

He said, 'I have only one small company, about fifty men, as the rest of the regiment that was stationed here were ordered to Arizona last week to fight Apaches, but we will put Samuel in the guardhouse and while this company lasts there won't any Indians get him. After that it won't make much difference to you and me whether they get him or not.' Continuing, he said, 'The other troops had no sooner gone to Arizona than a party of Utes from Colorado, headed by the renegade Ute Jack, came here and tried to get the Arapahoes to go on the warpath with them in Colorado. I started in to arrest Ute Jack, but he showed fight, hurt one or two of my men, then barricaded himself in a tepee and told us to get him if we could. I turned a Gatling gun loose and there wasn't anything worth mentioning left of Jack or the tepee. It stirred up a row, though, and Sharp Nose and his band were for cleaning us out at once. With the help they would have had from the bad element in Black Coal's band, they could have mighty near done it too, but Washakie came in on our side with the Shoshones and he and Black Coal had influence enough to stop it.'

The captain pondered for a moment and then continued, 'These devils were excited and restless all the week, but had just begun to settle down when here you come and ride right into Sharp Nose's camp to arrest Samuel. This is bound to stir them up again and what the result will be no one can tell. But say, Canton, I like your nerve, and if there is to be any fighting count me in, only I cannot let any of my men go outside of the post.'

It was comforting to me to know we had some one upon whom we could depend, and by the time I had Samuel in the guardhouse, the horses in the quartermaster's stable, and my three men in the company mess room getting breakfast, I began to feel better.

As soon as I had left the Indian camp with my prisoner, Sharp Nose had at once sent couriers to Black Coal, whose village was at the Forks five miles down the river, and to Washakie, whose village was several miles from the agency in another direction. The captain took me home with him and when we ap-

peared on the parade ground after breakfast, there
were at least five hundred warriors outside the post,
many with their war bonnets on, and all very much
excited. Washakie, with perhaps a dozen of the head
men of the Shoshones, and Black Coal with about the
same number of his band of Arapahoes had come into
the post, and were standing in two groups near the
flagstaff.

The captain and I walked over to them, shook hands
with Washakie and Black Coal, and then I began talking to them. First I showed my warrants for the arrest of the two Indians, which the interpreter read to
them.

Then turning to Black Coal, all the time talking
slowly through the interpreter, I said, 'I have been
ordered by the high court to come here and arrest these
two Indians and to take them to Buffalo to be punished for stealing cattle. If you or any of your band
interfere with me the Great Father at Washington will
not recognize you any longer as head chief of the
Arapahoes. I have one of the Indians, Samuel, in the
guardhouse now. You know who the other is and
where to find him. You send your men out to find him
and turn him over to me. Then tell all your warriors
to let me take both of them peaceably and I will always be your friend, and I will have the court make the
punishment as light as possible, but they must be
punished so they will be good Indians when they come
back.'

Black Coal took me by the hand and kept hold of it

until he could tell me that he was the big chief of the Arapahoes, that he was my friend, that he would bring in Beaver, the other Indian. Black Coal then sent six of his men away and inside of an hour they came back with Beaver. I put him in the guardhouse with Samuel and the first thing that Beaver wanted was the medicine bag and then claimed the pinto pony and saddle, which I promised to return to him. Samuel claimed the hat, which disposed of all the chattels in my possession belonging to the Indians.

I then returned to the parade ground and found there a courier from the agent, who said that Sharp Nose wanted to have a talk with me in the council house at the agency. It looked like a warm proposition for us to ride that mile through all those Indians. The captain said he could not send an escort outside of the post, and Black Coal said that he did not want to fight Sharp Nose just then. I was determined to know what Sharp Nose had to say, so my three men and I rode down alone. The Indians seemed to know what our errand was, for they scattered out on each side of the trail making a wide lane, and when we rode up to the council house Washakie was there to meet us. There were some two hundred Arapahoes of Sharp Nose's band outside as well, while inside the council house were the agent, with an interpreter, and Sharp Nose with about thirty villainous-looking bucks.

I left McClennan to hold the horses, while Chris Gross, Bill Glass, and myself went inside to hear what Sharp Nose had to say. There were no preliminaries in the way of a smoke, which ordinarily an Indian wants before he does any talking, for Sharp Nose was too angry. He began at once talking through the interpreter and the gist of his speech was that the white men had killed all the buffalo and elk which originally belonged to the Indians, and that now it was right for the Indians to kill the white man's cattle. In reply I made about the same talk I had made on the parade ground to Black Coal, but the more I talked the more vicious and angry Sharp Nose looked and acted. When I finished, he first offered twenty-five ponies if I would turn Samuel and Beaver loose. Of course, I refused to part with my prisoners and Sharp Nose promptly raised the bid to fifty ponies. Then, as I shook my head, he quickly came back with an offer of seventy-five of his best, many of them to be war ponies.

On my further declining any overtures in the shape of ponies, Sharp Nose almost lost control of himself, he was so mad. Putting his hand under his blanket as if to pull a six-shooter or a knife, he stepped towards me, while his men all spread out in a quarter-circle, with their hands under their blankets watching intently for any change in affairs. Four of the oldest Indians were armed with bows and arrows, a most dangerous weapon at close quarters when in the hands of an Indian, and they began pulling arrows from the quivers, feeling of the points to be sure they were sharp, until each of the four had half a dozen different arrows in his hands. I put my hand on my six-shooter and Gross and Glass pulled theirs clear from the scabbards.

At that moment Sharp Nose seemed to collect himself, stopped, raised one hand, looked me squarely in the eye and said, 'If you try to take Samuel and Beaver off the reservation I will kill and scalp you, and all your party.'

I answered, 'I am going to start with them in the morning for Buffalo. If you attempt to stop us or to interfere with us in any way, I will first kill them and then we will fight you as long as we have a cartridge.'

Sharp Nose then gave me a scowl and stalked out of the council house, followed by his band. My men and I followed right out so as to get with McClennan if there was to be any fighting, but we found that Black Coal had forestalled any designs that Sharp Nose may have had in that line by being there with about one hundred of his best men, and all well armed and mounted on their war horses, with McClennan's and my four horses in the center. They formed on each side and behind our party and saw us safely back to the post.

From the instant we first entered the council house until we were inside the post again had been like sitting on a powder barrel. Just one false move on the part of any of us, either white or Indian, would have been the spark that would have fired the powder, which would have meant death to us as well as the death of many of the Indians. Black Coal's act in being at the council house with his men showed how well he appreciated the situation and how binding he considered his promise made to me on the parade ground in the morning to be my friend.

I had now accomplished what I came for, the arrest of Samuel and Beaver, but how to get them out of that country and back to Buffalo seemed a greater task than anything up to that time. There were two ways that we could go, one to take the State road south to Rawlins, then the Union Pacific east to Rock Creek, and from there by stage north two hundred and fifty miles to Buffalo. This would necessitate leaving the horses and saddles at Washakie, which I disliked to do. The other route was to go back down Little Wind River through all the Indian camps over the trail we came. I talked it over with my men and we all decided that if Sharp Nose intended to put his threat into execution the Indians could get us even better in the stage than when on horseback, and that the bolder way was the better, so we chose the Little Wind River trail, believing that if we could make the first twenty-five miles to Black Coal's village we would stand a good show to win out. I had two more in my party to provide horses for on the return trip, so I still kept the pinto pony for Beaver to ride and got Black Coal to lend me a pony on which to mount Samuel. When we rode up to the guardhouse early next morning to receive the prisoners, who should be sitting on the ground near by but Mollie! She had come into the post about ten o'clock the night before and had stayed near the guardhouse all night to make sure that Samuel was not moved without her seeing him again.

She at once came up to me and said, 'Mr. Canton, I want you to let me go to Buffalo with Sam.'

I answered, 'No, Mollie, I can't let you go. I have all I can care for now, and if Sharp Nose attacks us, you might get killed with the rest of us.'

Mollie answered, 'You told Sharp Nose that if he tried to stop you, you would kill Sam and Beaver. If you kill Sam I don't want to live. I want to be near him. I won't make any trouble. Sharp Nose is a bad Indian and he got Sam to kill cattle. I know Sam has to be punished, but I must go with him to help him. He can't speak English. I will be interpreter.'

She kept on begging so piteously that finally I told her she might go. Then such a change came over her. At first she had been in tears, but now she was almost like a child, she was so happy. She had been at Carlisle long enough so that she had become more demonstrative than Indians are naturally, and taking my hand she began drawing me towards the guardhouse, and when inside with Sam the scene was quite affecting. After a few minutes I handcuffed my prisoners and put them on their horses, tying their feet under the horses, being determined that neither of them should give me the slip while going down the river. McClennan led the two horses the prisoners were on, Mollie led the pack horses, thus leaving Gross, Glass, and myself to do the fighting if the Indians attempted any surprise.

Soon after leaving the post, Indians could be seen on each side, three or four hundred yards away, riding about even with us, two hundred or more on each side. I tried to get Mollie to ride out to them and explain that if any attack was made I was fully determined to kill Samuel and Beaver the first thing.

But Mollie said, 'No, Mr. Canton, I am afraid to go. They never would let me come back to Sam if they once got hold of me. Besides, every Indian on the reservation knows that you intend to kill Sam and Beaver if they interfere with you.'

The Indians kept along with us, but off a little distance, for twenty miles, until they passed the camp of Sharp Nose.

A short distance below the camp the river went into a canyon and the trail there was just wide enough between the river and the bluff for a pack horse to travel. Just at the entrance to this canyon an Indian was squatted in the trail with his blanket drawn over his head. As I rode up I thought this was where the trouble was to begin, but I also made up my mind to put on a bold front and take the initiative. As I approached, the Indian sprang to his feet, threw back his blanket, and caught my bridle rein. The Indian was Sharp Nose. As soon as I saw who it was I gave him a jab in the face with my Winchester, spurred my horse, and literally rode him down. Sharp Nose rolled over out of the trail and the party all rode by in single file, Glass and Gross, who were bringing up the rear, being ready to kill him if he made a threatening motion. But he did not. He seemed to be completely cowed. After we were well past Sharp Nose, the whole camp commenced a most mournful chant, which Mollie explained was the death song for Samuel and Beaver.

At Black Coal's village five miles below, Black Coal
was on the lookout for us and seemed glad that we had
come that far in safety. He gave me two trusty Indians to act as scouts until we were through the mountains, so none of Sharp Nose's band could ambush us,
and we kept on for another ten miles into the open
country before going into camp. Black Coal also told
Mollie to return with the scouts, but when the time
came for the scouts to turn back she developed senti-
ments of her own and told me she was going to stay
with Sam as long as she could. From this camp to
Buffalo, about one hundred and sixty miles, we made
easy rides and landed the prisoners safely in jail.

It was to be nearly four months before court convened, so my wife arranged a back room in our house
for Mollie and saw that she had her meals, and most of
the day Mollie was with Sam. At the trial she acted
as interpreter. I told Judge Blair of the promise I had
made to Black Coal and the judge gave the lightest
sentence he could, one year in the penitentiary at
Joliet, Illinois, with the time off that they had served
in jail — about four months, making about eight
months at Joliet. One Sunday night while they were
in jail I was alone in my office and at ten o'clock I went
into the jail to see that the prisoners were all in their
cells, and to lock the jail for the night. Bill Booth, a
condemned murderer, and a burglar were in one cell,
as we were crowded for room. When I came to their
cell the door was shut, but I could get no reply when
I called their names. The 'trusty' in the corridor

said they were in there, but were probably asleep. Samuel's cell was opposite, and on looking around I noticed him making signals. Then he began at once talking the 'sign language' and told me that the 'trusty' had secured a wrench with which he had taken the burrs off the bolts that fastened the hinges to the cell door, let the prisoners out, and then had replaced the bolts so that at first glance the door looked all right; that the prisoners at that time were in an iron tank over the cells, which supplied water for the jail.

I climbed up quietly and upon opening the lid of the tank found them sitting in the water up to their necks. The murderer showed fight, but a blow on the head with my six-shooter settled him. Then I made the burglar pull the stunned man out of the tank and, as soon as he recovered his senses, made him get the man down on the floor and into his cell.

This act showed that Samuel's heart was in the right place and that he bore no grudge for being arrested. McDermott took Samuel and Beaver to Joliet and arranged with the warden to allow them to keep their long hair, which is an Indian's pride, and put them at work caring for the horses inside the walls, which they naturally learned quickly.

When McDermott left Buffalo with them Mollie was broken-hearted, but Mrs. Canton comforted her all she could, and the next day Mollie saddled her horse and started for the reservation. She had shown herself a trump through all her troubles and proved that human nature is the same the world over and that her love for Sam was just as strong and perfect in its way as that of any white woman for her husband. About every six weeks while Sam was in Joliet, Mollie would ride the two hundred miles from the reservation to Buffalo and stay one or two days with Mrs. Canton to learn what had been heard of Sam, never failing to bring something for Mrs. Canton. At one time she brought a beautiful buffalo robe with Indian pictures worked in porcupine quills. The next trip she gave a fine saddle pony, which Mrs. Canton rode for years. At another time she brought handsome beadwork, and often a string of mountain trout caught at her last camp on the mountains a few miles from town, all simple tokens of her good will.

Soon after Samuel and Beaver were arrested, I had the opportunity to repay Black Coal in part for his kindness at the council house. A white man called Big George, a noted horse thief, stole some sixty-odd horses from Black Coal's own bunch and crossed the Big Horn River with them, close to where I was camped the first night after leaving Fort Washakie with my prisoners. I heard the horses crossing but could do nothing at that time. In fact, I did not know they were stolen. But as soon as I had Samuel and Beaver safe in Buffalo, Deputy Gross and I started into the Big Horn Mountains to intercept them if possible, and learn where they were from. We caught them at the Waun boys' cabin, about fifty miles southwest of Buffalo. Big George objected to being arrested and was killed by Gross. Gross and I returned the horses to Black Coal, and during the rest of his life he was always ready to do anything in his power for me.

When the time of Samuel and Beaver expired at Joliet, Major McClaughrey, the warden, bought each a suit of clothes and a ticket to Rawlins, Wyoming, gave each of them an open letter, 'To Whom it May Concern,' etc., and started them for home. On her last trip to Buffalo Mollie had learned from Mrs. Canton about the date that Sam and Beaver would reach Rawlins, and when passenger train Number Three pulled in, she was on the platform, devoted as ever, to meet Sam.

The arrest and conviction of the two Arapahoes had the effect of stopping all cattle stealing by the Indians. They appeared to have a horror of going to jail and when they found that I wanted to be square with them, they never failed to pay me a visit when in the country, and often gave me valuable information about what was going on in the mountains that I could not have gotten any other way.

CHAPTER IV

THE JOHNSON COUNTY WAR

ONE day a band of about a hundred and twenty-five Cheyenne Indians, on their way to visit the Arapahoes and Shoshones, had camped on an island near Fort McKinney, a government post about a mile above Buffalo. In the evening two Indians came down to Buffalo to see me, leading a pack horse. I recognized them at once. They were Dull Knife and Two Moons, the two Indian chiefs who had led the Cheyenne raid through Kansas, Nebraska, and South Dakota in 1878. I made each one of them a present of a pipe and some smoking tobacco, and they rode away together. I thought no more about them until I was aroused from sleep about two o'clock next morning by a little twelve-year-old German girl named Mollie Fisher. She said the Indians were on the warpath. I hurriedly dressed and called one of my deputies. We grabbed our Winchesters and revolvers and the girl guided us to where she had seen the Indians, which was near her father's house.

There was a full moon, all was quiet, and we could see no Indians. Finally we found a tepee and three ponies picketed out near the banks of Clear Creek just below a rocky ravine near the limits of the town. After looking around I found an Indian squatted in the sage brush with his blanket over him and his head between his knees. I pulled the blanket off of him and helped him upon his feet. It was Dull Knife, one of the Cheyenne chiefs. His hair was matted with blood which had soaked through the blanket.

When I asked him what the trouble was, he merely pointed to the ravine and said, 'Heap fight.'

We went down in the bottom of the ravine and found Two Moons lying on his back, unconscious from the loss of blood. We got cold water from the creek close by and poured on his head and face, and soon revived him. The rocks and boulders for fifty feet around where they had been fighting were covered with blood. They had camped there alone for the night and had managed to get whiskey from some one. There already was a bitter feeling between these two Indians. The liquor added fuel to the flame and primed them for the bloody contest. Two Moons wanted to succeed Dull Knife as chief, but as Dull Knife had been the war chief for many years, he would not surrender the honors to another, although the tribe wanted Two Moons, as he was young and a great fighter. The result was that they got a few drinks under the belts and decided to settle their superiority by fighting a duel to a finish.

They fought with the old buffalo-skinning knife which is a murderous weapon, with a blade from six to nine inches in length. Both Indians were literally cut to pieces. Two Moons was young and the more powerful, as he was about six feet and weighed about two hundred pounds, while Dull Knife was slender, but quick and active as a panther. It must have been a battle royal. While this was a savage custom, some-how this primitive fashion of settling a dispute be-tween the leaders strikes me as a better test of bravery than by following the more modern, civilized way; that is, to have others do the fighting while the chiefs re-main in the rear of the battle in comparative safety.

I sent a messenger up to my old friend Frank Ger-ard, Government scout at Fort McKinney, and told him what had happened. He sent for Dr. John A. Summars, Post Surgeon, and ordered an ambulance to take the wounded Indians to the hospital. The band of Cheyennes all followed them down. The Indians, with the exception of one squaw, paid no attention to Dull Knife, but would not allow the surgeon or any one else to touch Two Moons, whom they had taken to their own camp and had treated by a medicine man. Dull Knife was placed in the ambulance and taken to the hospital. When Dr. Summars examined him he found seventeen deep knife wounds in his neck, back, and side. The knife in many places had been driven to the hilt. He treated the wounds and sewed them up, but had no idea the Indian would live.

In two or three days the Cheyennes all left for their homes on the Rosebud in Montana, taking Two Moons with them. Dull Knife's squaw had been in a separate camp alone. When the other Indians all left she re-mained in her camp with two saddle ponies and one pack horse. Early one morning Dr. Summars called at the hospital to see his patient and found Dull Knife gone. The squaw had taken his saddle pony up to the

gate of the hospital, helped the wounded Indian down-
stairs in the night and put him on his pony. They both
struck the Rosebud trail and pulled out for their home.
Dull Knife and Two Moons were both living the last
I heard of them.

In 1886 I was strongly urged by the citizens of Johnson County to accept the office as sheriff for a third
term. But as my little herd of cattle and my farm
needed my attention, I retired from public life and
moved out to my ranch with my young wife and little
daughter Ruby.

I have never felt that an officer deserves any great
amount of credit for doing his duty, but when I turned
the sheriff's office over to my successor, E. U. Snider, I
presented him with a record that I was not ashamed
of. During the four years that I had served as sheriff
of Johnson County, I had served and returned every
criminal writ and indictment issued from the courts of
our county, and not a single return showed 'not found.'
Owing to the immense amount of criminal work that
we had to do, I thought this was a remarkable record,
and I have always been proud of it.

The next two years I spent at home with my family.
My ranch was located in a valley under the peaks of the
Big Horn Mountains in the finest climate in the world.
My wife was very fond of horseback riding and enjoyed being out with me. I think those were the hap-
piest days of my life. I had accumulated about five
hundred head of fine cattle and made a success of farming. I had a prior right to an irrigating ditch which

had plenty of water, and raised an excellent quality of wheat, oats, barley, and hay, that always commanded the top price in the markets.

E. U. Snider, who succeeded me as sheriff, did not make a success of the office. He was a good man and a big-hearted fellow, but was not sufficiently aggressive to make good as a Western sheriff. In those days, saloons and gambling games were allowed a license in the towns and the sheriff did the collecting, and was responsible to the county for the funds after the license was issued. Sheriff Snider generally delivered the license to the saloon-keepers and gamblers on their promise to pay for it in a few days. The consequences were that they never paid, which put the sheriff in the hole and he was compelled to pay the county several thousand dollars for license money due. The criminal element of the county was also handled in a loose and easy-going way, and it soon began to take advantage of the situation. In a short time there was organized the most systematic and powerful gang of cattle thieves ever known in the history of the United States, which finally resulted in the Wyoming cattle war, or rustler war, as it has been generally called.

There were a number of large cattle ranches in Johnson County, on Powder River, Crazy Woman Creek, Tongue River, and in the Big Horn Mountains, owned by Englishmen of note who had invested large fortunes in that county and were prominent members of the Wyoming Stock Association. Morton and Richard Frewen owned the '76 Ranch. Horace Plunkett, who

A RANCH ON THE PLAINS

was made famous during the Irish civil trouble in England and Ireland, owned the E K Ranch. Stewart Wortly, son-in-law of Admiral Schley, U.S.N., was interested in the C̲ (bar C) Ranch. William Haywood, an English writer of note, owned the L7 brand. Other prominent men, such as John Clay, Jr., and Henry Blair, of Chicago, United States Senators, Francis E. Warren and J. M. Carey, of Wyoming, Ex-Governor George Baxter, of Wyoming, and many others too numerous to mention, were owners of cattle ranches.

Besides these there were hundreds of other honest men who owned from two hundred and fifty to a thousand head of cattle each. The large ranch owners did not stay at their ranches themselves, except through the shipping season, but depended entirely upon their foremen to look after the business and allowed them to select their own cowboys. These foremen were paid high salaries, and while they had nothing to do through the long winter months except to draw their salaries and keep the ice broken in the water holes so that the range stock could get water, their wages were never reduced, but remained the same the year around.

But the mistake of selecting the wrong man for foreman was made in many cases by the large cattle-owners. There was a class of men who had drifted into that country who were 'would-be cowboys,' and many of them had been driven out of Montana by Granville Stuart and the vigilance committees in 1879, and many others had had to leave Texas for cattle stealing. Not knowing the record of these men and thinking they

were like the majority of cowboys, loyal and true to
their employers, they secured many of their foremen
from this class. These foremen then selected their
men from the criminal element of their own caliber,
and began starting brands of their own. They would
ride the range through the winter months on horses
owned by their employers, and when they found a calf
following a cow that belonged to the man that was paying them wages, they would brand the calf if it was old
enough to wean, separate it from its mother and turn
it loose. At other times they would brand the calf,
then run the cow off in some canyon, shoot her down,
and leave the meat for the gray wolves and coyotes.

Each man carried a small iron rod on his saddle,
which he called a 'running iron,' used in blotching and
changing brands. The thief, or rustler as he called
himself, which was a picturesque, gentlemanly name
for a cattle thief, would always select a brand, which he
would record in his own name, that would cover most
any brand on the range. He would change the ear
mark, and with the use of the running iron, could
change the old brand so that you could not tell what
the original brand was, except in one way, and that
was to kill the animal, take the hide off, and look at the
inside of the hide which would show a white welt, or
scar, so plainly that you could easily tell what the
original brand was. The new brand would not show
on the inside of the hide. I secured evidence in this
way at one time in Montana and convicted three cattle
thieves.

The conditions in Johnson County grew from bad to worse. The ranch owners discharged their foremen who had 'double-crossed' them, and they also fired a great many of their men. The Stock Association 'blackballed' the whole bunch and signed an agreement not to allow any of them to work with the outfit of any member of the Association. The rustlers then banded together and worked the range with pack outfits, in defiance of the laws of the territory and the rules of range work among honest men. There were many honest foremen of cow ranches in that country, such men as Fred Hess, foreman of the '76 Ranch, Frank Laberteaux of the Hoe Ranch, Billie Irvine and Charley Ford of the T A Ranch, Jim Craig, and many others, who stood for law and order and had fought the cattle and horse thieves from the beginning. They also had cowboys of the old school under them whom they could count on under any and all circumstances, but the lawless element had gotten such a start that the officers of the county appeared to be absolutely unable to check them.

In 1888 E. U. Snider retired from the sheriff's office and W. H. Angus, commonly called Red Angus, was elected sheriff. I again accepted a position with the Wyoming Stock Association as range inspector with a commission as Deputy United States Marshal. In a short time I had secured positive evidence in many cases for cattle stealing. The thieves were arrested and brought into court, but it was almost impossible to convict a rustler. The jury was summoned from the

body of citizens of the county and friends and sympathizers of the thieves would always manage to get on
the jury and turn the defendants loose as fast as we
arrested them.

Judge Saufley of Kentucky, who was District Judge
at that time, in the trial of a case of six men for cattle
stealing who were acquitted, reprimanded the jury in
open court and told them that they ought to be prosecuted themselves for turning those men loose. He said
that they were the most guilty bunch that ever walked
out of a courtroom. It finally got to the point where
the honest citizens were afraid to testify against a
rustler for fear that their stock would all be stolen and
probably their homes burned.

The change in the sheriff's office did not improve the
situation so far as making convictions in cattle-stealing
cases was concerned. The rustlers got such a foothold
that the trial was invariably a farce.

This state of affairs lasted for several years, growing
worse all the time. Red Angus was elected sheriff in
1890. There were many common cowpunchers in the
rustlers' band who in early days were glad to get a job
of 'wrangling horses' at twenty-five dollars per month,
who now claimed from two hundred and fifty to five
hundred cattle each on the range.

About the only market they had for these stolen
cattle in Johnson County was to sell them to an old
merchant, who had a large supply store in Buffalo.
This old man was a Scotchman who had made a fortune
in the early days in Wyoming, about Elk Mountain,

on tie contracts with the Union Pacific Railroad Company when they were building through Wyoming. He then moved to Buffalo and started a large store. He made a success for a time, and I always felt very kindly towards the old man myself. But he made the mistake of his life when he commenced dealing with the rustlers and furnishing a market for their stolen property. He bought the cattle cheap, but he had to ship them to the Eastern markets to get any money out of them. He made his shipments to Omaha, but the burnt and blotched brands on the cattle would not stand the inspection of the vigilant stock inspectors stationed at that shipping point. The stolen cattle were taken away from him and confiscated. I understand that he lost from fifty to seventy-five thousand dollars on his deal with the rustlers.

In 1891 two rustlers, John Tisdale and Ranger Jones, were shot and killed by unknown parties some fifteen miles south of Buffalo. They had both been shot from ambush and on different days and at different points on the county road. It was claimed by the rustling fraternity and the opponents of the stock men that the Stock Association had these men killed, that the two men were law-abiding citizens and innocent of any offense against the stock law. If this were true it seems strange that they at once assumed that both were killed by the contrivance of the Stock Association.

Relations between the stock men and the rustlers had been strained almost to breaking point. Rumors of vigilance committees and lynching parties current on all sides had made the rustlers suspicious and nervous and they had gradually been drawing together at various centers in the county for mutual protection and profit. When the news of the death of Tisdale and Jones reached them from town they all flocked into Buffalo in a state of great excitement. The Stock Association was denounced as the instigator of the murder and the names of prominent stock men in town were openly connected with the crime.

My family, at this time, was in Chicago visiting relatives. I had been confined to my bed in Buffalo for several weeks with a severe attack of inflammatory rheumatism, and was intending to go to Chicago as soon as I was able to ride on the railroad. Fred Hess, foreman of the '76 Ranch, was also in Buffalo with his family at that time. No attempt was made by the officers to trace the murderers of Tisdale and Jones beyond the scene of the tragedy.

It was whispered about among the rustlers and their friends that I was the man who killed them both, and they at once decided on a plot to assassinate me, which failed to materialize. I then called upon a bunch of the leaders of the rustlers and demanded that they prefer charges against me in order that I might meet and refute the slander. This, after considerable hesitation, was done. I surrendered to the sheriff, had a trial, and I proved by a large number of the best citizens of the county that I was in Buffalo every hour of the day on which Tisdale was killed. In the Jones case the evidence was exactly the same. The prosecution had no evidence and I had a perfect defense without any question of doubt. The case was dismissed, but the rustlers were not satisfied. While I do not believe there was a single man among them that believed that I was guilty of the charge, they wanted some excuse for getting me out of the way, and I knew they intended to do it the first time they got the drop on me. They also wanted to kill Fred Hess, because he had taken a prominent part in having them prosecuted.

The rustlers all knew that I intended to go to Chicago to join my family, but they expected me to leave Buffalo for the railroad in the night, so they guarded every road out of Buffalo each night, thinking they would get a chance to ambush me as I came out. I had just received a telegram to the effect that my wife was ill in Chicago, and decided to leave at once for Gillette, the nearest railroad station on the Burlington. I advised Fred Hess to go with me, which he decided to do, as I thought he would be in great danger if he remained in Buffalo alone.

Next morning about nine o'clock Fred Hess, Sam Southerland, a cowboy, and myself, all well armed and on good horses, rode down through the main street of Buffalo. There was a big crowd of rustlers standing on the streets, but they were so astonished to think that we would ride out of town in broad daylight in plain sight of them all, that they looked foolish and said nothing. But before we were out of sight I looked back and saw them mounting their horses. We took the main traveled stage road to Gillette, down Clear Creek. I had no fear that the rustlers would follow us up and attack us in the rear even with their large numbers. But I realized that our danger lay in allowing them to get ahead of us and prepare an ambush for us to ride into. I was satisfied that this was their game, and I recalled that there was a short cut on the trail that ran through the Red Hills and down Crazy Woman Creek and intercepted the road we were on at Powder River. I was satisfied this would be the trail the rustlers would take if they tried to cut us off and reach Powder River ahead of us, where they knew we had to come in order to make the Gillette Crossing.

In passing the old L X Ranch about eight miles below Buffalo near the road, we saw some eight or ten of the rustlers there with their horses saddled. I presume they had been on guard there all the night before waiting for us. They took a good look at us as we passed and I am sure they recognized us, for they knew all three of us by sight. We got a position where we could watch them a few minutes with our glasses as soon as we were out of sight. The rustlers had mounted their horses and were heading full speed in the direction of the Red Hills. We held a short conference and agreed that our only hope for safety was to ride, and ride hard. It was about sixty miles to Powder River. If we could make that ahead of the rustlers we were safe; if not, we were 'in for it.' Our horses were in good shape and we put them to the test. We crossed Powder River ahead of the rustlers, then made an easy ride to Gillette. I learned afterwards that when we struck Powder River we were only about fifteen minutes ahead of a large bunch of rustlers who had made the cut-off through the Red Hills. It is not my nature to complain or feel resentment, but as our horses galloped steadily along in this race for the crossing, I could not keep from thinking of the cause of this hatred on the part of the outlaws. It would have been easy for me to have compromised with them when I was sheriff, but as I had been uncompromising and relentless, and they were tacitly encouraged by a succeeding sheriff, they were getting even with me.

When I reached Chicago I found my wife and two little daughters all down with diphtheria. I remained in Chicago all winter to care for them. We had a very serious time and lost one of our little girls.

In April I was requested by the Wyoming Stock Association to return to Cheyenne. My wife and little daughter Ruby had almost recovered from their illness and I left them with relatives and came out to Cheyenne, Wyoming. This was in the spring of 1892. I found a large number of cattle owners in Cheyenne from Johnson and other counties in Wyoming, that had organized an expedition to go to Johnson County, for the purpose of rounding up what cattle they had left on the range and shipping them to the Eastern markets. They had also secured warrants for some ten or twelve of the leaders of the rustler band in Johnson County.

They requested me to join the party and take

charge of the criminal warrants for the arrest of certain rustlers. I consented to do this, as my interests in Johnson County needed looking after badly.

Major Wolcott, a cattle owner and an ex-army officer, was placed in command of the expedition. As they expected to have trouble in arresting some of the rustlers they had secured the services of some brave and experienced officers from the Indian Territory. I will mention the names of a few of these men: Tom Smith, a famous Deputy United States Marshal from Indian Territory and Texas; Dave Booker, Chief of Police and Deputy United States Marshal at Ardmore, Indian Territory, for many years; Buck Garrett, a well-known officer, later sheriff at Ardmore, Oklahoma; George Tucker; Bill Little; and several more officers who had always made good. The rest of the party were Wyoming cattle men, such as Fred Hess, Billie Irvine, Frank Laberteaux, and others. There were forty-two in all.

In order that the rustlers should know nothing about this movement and escape to the mountains before we got into their rendezvous, we had to work very quietly in getting started. We secured a special engine and several cars for our men and equipment, and entrained at Cheyenne at night. We then made a remarkably fast run to a point out west near Casper, Wyoming, where we detrained on the prairie. After getting our commissary supplies, ammunition, and other equipment all in the wagons, five hundred rounds of ammunition for rifle and revolver were issued to each man to be carried on the saddle. We then mounted our horses and started out on the campaign.

Major Wolcott had detailed two or three men, in addition to the drivers, to stay with the wagons, and gave orders for the mounted men to make a forced march across the country to Powder River about eighty miles north. We had received reliable information to the effect that the stronghold of the rustlers was at the K C Ranch on Powder River, and that most of the rustlers for whom we had warrants were at this ranch, and had been there all winter. April weather in Wyoming is always bad. At this time a light snow covered the ground, which made it difficult for fast marching, and the men and horses were soft. However, we made good time by riding all night, and reached the K C Ranch before daylight.

This ranch house was a double log cabin built of heavy pine timber. The rustlers had cut portholes along each side, which made an excellent fort for the protection of the defenders during an attack from the outside. A few men with a supply of ammunition, plenty of water, and something to eat could stand off a large force on the outside indefinitely. We surrounded the house, each man taking a position about forty or fifty yards from the building, and waited for daylight. Just after daybreak a man came out of the house with a water bucket in his hand, and started towards the creek in the direction of where I was stationed with several men behind a small barn. When the man with the bucket had approached near to me, I covered him with my Winchester, and called to him to advance to me at once. He was scared almost to death, but he did not give any alarm. He walked over to me under our guns, and upon being questioned he told me that he and his partner had been trapping and skinning wolves; that he was not connected in any way with the rustlers, and had stopped at this place the day before. He said his partner was in the house and pointed to an old light wagon near the house which he said was his. I was satisfied from his appearance and talk that he was telling me the truth. I then asked him how many men there were in the house and who they were. He said, that when he and his partner first came to the ranch the day before, there was a large bunch of men there, but that they all left the evening before except two, Nate Champion and Nick Ray, and that they were both in the house. I told this man to go back into the house and tell Champion and Ray that we had the place surrounded; that we had warrants for their arrest for cattle stealing and demanded their surrender; if they refused to comply with my demand, for him and his partner to come out at once, and we would not fire a shot until they were out of danger. He then went back into the house.

In a few minutes he and his partner came out, walking very fast. He had delivered my message, which was answered by a volley from the house. As soon as the two men had reached a place of safety behind our firing line, the command was given by Major Wolcott to commence firing. Nick Ray was shot and killed, I think, about the second volley. He had taken a position behind the door-facing and was firing out of the door. The smoke from his gun showed his position and he was shot dead and fell across the doorstep with his head and shoulders on the inside of the building. Champion was shooting out of the portholes as fast as he could burn ammunition. By the way, Nate Champion was the only man among the rustlers that I considered a dead-game man. He was an expert shot with a rifle and came near getting several of our men. The only thing we could do was to pour lead into the portholes, but as fast as we drove him from one position, he would open up from another. Almost three hours after the fight started, orders had been given to cease firing.

A man in a wagon driving two horses and a young fellow with him drove down to the K C Ranch. When he saw armed men, he whipped his team to a dead run and crossed the creek on a little bridge near where some of our men were stationed. He was recognized at once as Jack Flag, the most notorious rustler in the county. He was ordered to surrender, but paid no attention to the command, and drove his team full speed on the road toward Buffalo. Several shots were fired at him, but missed on account of shooting through the timber along the creek, and by the time we had mounted our horses, which were some distance away, Jack Flag had got the horses loose, jumped on one of them, and escaped, going in the direction of Buffalo. We went out and brought his wagon

back, took off the front wheels, fastened the coupling
pole on tight, got some posts and tied them onto the
hind axle, in an upright position for breastworks. Then
we tied up a bunch of dry hay in front of the posts, and
two men pushed this arrangement up against the building and set it on fire, while the rest of us were shooting into the portholes. It was not long before the dry
pine timber caught fire and the house was in flames.
Champion was determined not to surrender. He came
out fighting and died game. If he had been fighting in
a good cause, he would have been a hero.

Our wagons had pulled in. After we had something
to eat, which we were badly in need of, we released the
two men whom we had captured at the ranch, and after
we had paid them one hundred dollars for burning up
their bedding, in the house, they went on their way. A
big supply of ammunition was issued to each man.
Then we received orders to march to Buffalo, which
was fifty miles north.

We left Powder River after dark. The wagons were
left behind to follow up. We had no moon to guide us
and the night would have been very dark had it not
been for the snow on the ground. When we reached
Poison Creek near Dick Carr's ranch we heard a shot
as we were crossing a flat country covered with grease-
wood brush, and our advance guard discovered the dim
forms of horsemen ahead of us. We dismounted immediately, threw skirmishers out, and formed a firing line
to be ready for attack. But the parties disappeared and
did not show up any more. We found out later that this

was a bunch of rustlers that Jack Flag, who had made his escape at the K C Ranch, had gotten together and taken down on the trail to attack us from ambush under cover of darkness, and the shot we heard was fired accidentally by one of his own men. They knew this shot would disclose their position to us and I presume they went to the brush. We made a hard ride that night. When we reached the 卅 ranch fourteen miles south of Buffalo some of our men, who were not accustomed to the hard service that we had experienced in the last few days, insisted on the party stopping at this ranch for a rest. We then held a conference. I objected strenuously to this move and insisted that we get into Buffalo as soon as possible for the following reasons: That more than two thirds of the people of the town were our intimate friends, and that we could explain the true situation to them; that they would not only assist us with their influence, but would join our party if we needed them. We could then keep our headquarters at Buffalo until we had rounded up our stock and arrested the rustlers. On the other hand, if we stopped at the 卅 ranch this would give the rustlers and their sympathizers a chance to stir up the entire country against us, and then we would have not only the one hundred and twenty-five rustlers to fight, but that many others would line up against us, for they did not know up to this time who we were nor who was in our party.

Fred Hess, W. J. Clark, Charley Ford, and others who lived in Johnson County approved of all I said. While talking, Jim Craig and John Pierce, two of our friends, rode up to us with a message from some of our people in Buffalo requesting us not to come into town at that time for fear of a battle in the town that might result in women and children getting hurt. They also said that Arapaho Brown, Jack Flag, and other agitators were stirring up the people in every way possible, and that they thought the rustlers would all come into Buffalo. Our friends meant all right, but they did not know the outlaws in that country as well as I did, and did not understand that up to that time we had the situation well in hand, and that we could get into Buffalo without having to fire a shot, establish headquarters, then the only fighting we might have to do would probably be something like the affair at the K C Ranch in arresting the outlaws that we had warrants for.

But the old saying that your friends sometimes hurt you worse than your enemies proved true in this case. We had only had one meal in thirty-six hours and some of our men were very badly worn out. The party voted to stop at the ranch. Major Wolcott gave his consent and made the mistake of his life.

We then pulled into the ranch, unsaddled our horses and put them into a corral, which had a small stream of water running through it, a good barn, and plenty of hay and grain. I then suggested to Major Wolcott that we build a temporary breastworks at the ranch building and dig rifle pits or trenches on a little hill about one hundred and fifty yards west of the ranch, and prepare for a siege. We all got busy and dug

trenches on this hill which covered the country around
for about eight hundred yards in every direction. The
trenches were built about fifty feet long, a hollow
square in the center with the four trenches extending
around the square, sufficient to hold fifteen or twenty
men. We built breastworks at the ranch building from
heavy pine slabs. Then we killed a beef, put the meat
in the house, and filled two barrels with drinking water,
which were also put in the house. We were satisfied
that the rustlers south of us would capture our wagons
and supplies, which afterwards proved true, but we
had plenty of ammunition and we found a big lot of
Irish potatoes in the cellar, also coffee and some flour.
By dark we had our fortifications in good shape, and
after getting supper we sent out outposts on guard
duty and the rest of us rolled up in our blankets on the
floor and were soon lost to the world.

About four o'clock the next morning, one of our
guards came in and awoke Major Wolcott, and reported that he had counted eighty riders passing in
through the front gate of the T A Ranch pasture on the
road from Buffalo to the T A Ranch, and that they had
all disappeared in the darkness, and that he thought
they were getting positions in the low hills surrounding
the ranch. Every one was quietly aroused from sleep
and ordered to get his clothes on. As soon as we were
dressed, the cook was put to work getting breakfast.
The outposts were all ordered in, and as soon as we had
a hot breakfast with plenty of black coffee, a detail of
fifteen men was placed on duty in the trenches on the

hill. Two men were stationed at the stable to attend to the horses; the guards who had been up all night were relieved from duty, that they might get the much-needed rest. We then filled our belts with ammunition and saw that our rifles were in good shape. Just about good daylight firing commenced from the hills in every direction at long range, from six hundred to eight hundred yards, and continued constantly for about half an hour. We had not yet fired a shot, as we were in no hurry to waste our ammunition and could see nothing to shoot at except a puff of smoke from the black powder that they used. With the aid of our field glasses we could plainly see the position of the enemy. They had dug holes in the soft bank in the bad lands around the ranch and were keeping well under cover. They shot into the ranch house and our breastworks, but were doing no damage except they occasionally dropped bullets in the corral among our horses and wounded several of them.

The best rifle we had in those days was the 45–70 Winchester, the 40–82 and the 38–56 magazine gun. The longest range for this gun was from six hundred to seven hundred yards. We were armed with this rifle and I presume they had the same kind of gun. But some man of their party had a rifle of larger caliber and greater penetration. The reports sounded to me like the old Sharps fifty-caliber that we formerly used on the plains and called the buffalo gun. This gun would hold up steady eight hundred yards and several times penetrated our breastworks, but did no particular harm. As we had not yet fired a shot the rustlers got a little closer and about a dozen men were seen riding along the slope of a hill about six hundred yards away in plain view. We thought this a good time to remind them that we were still living. We got the range, I think, very accurately. About twenty-five shots were fired in one volley. One saddle was emptied and two horses went down. The rest of them scattered to the hills for cover and they were very careful after that to keep out of range of our guns, but kept up a continuous range firing all day. In the evening two of our friends, old cowboys, had managed to get through the rustlers' line and joined our party at the ranch, and remained with us through the fight. One of them, Phil DuFresne, who had formerly run a road ranch in the Big Horn Basin, told us that the rustlers had sent a messenger to every settlement in the country telling them that our party were all new residents of the Territory and that we were put there for the purpose of driving out all the actual settlers and burning their houses, and all kinds of ridiculous stories. He said the honest settlers did not take any stock in these reports, but that a large per cent of the people were very much excited and a good many were joining the rustlers.

The firing from the rustlers continued at intervals all night. There was considerable snow on the ground and we could distinguish an object at some distance. Some of the rustlers would crawl up near to us under cover of darkness and fire on us. We would then return the fire and shoot at the flash of their guns.

Next morning at daylight we could see the number of rustlers had increased. We had breakfast, then sent fifteen men up to the trenches to relieve the old detail. In going from the ranch up to the trenches and returning we were in the open all the time for a hundred and fifty yards and under heavy fire from the enemy. But we had lost no men up to this time. About 10 A.M. of the second day, one of the rustlers had crawled up a gulch and dug a hole in a bank in which he concealed himself, about three hundred yards from the ranch. None of them had ever ventured that close before. This fellow commenced firing at the east end of our breastworks and shooting uncomfortably close to some of our men, then he would do several 'stunts,' stick his hat up on the end of his gun, etc.

I directed our men behind the breast works to keep quiet and not fire until I gave the order. Then I got a large augur, and crawled up into the attic of the ranch house. The ceiling was very low, but by getting down on my knees I soon bored out a large porthole through the soft pine logs. This gave me a good view of the sharpshooter in the hills. I could see his head very plainly through the sights of my rifle. I then directed the men below to take good aim and fire when I counted three. Twelve shots were fired in one volley. We literally covered the fellow up in dirt and dust, and he went out of sight. I don't know whether we killed him or not. There is one thing sure, he never showed up any more. When I fired the shot from the top of the building, the rustlers could see the smoke from my

portholes in the roof. They immediately began shooting by volleys at the roof of the house and soon shot
the shingles all to pieces. I was lucky to get down
from this place without being hit. In the afternoon the
rustlers started to dig post holes on the north side of
the ranch off quite a distance. I think their plan was
to stretch barbed wire around the ranch so that we
could not get out. Our men from the trenches on the
hill then opened up on them with such a hot fire that
they went to cover like a lot of quail and abandoned
their plan of stretching the wire.

There was not a time either in daylight or night but
what we could have cut through their lines and come
out with our entire party, and we all knew it, but as we
had gone to the trouble to build fortifications and they
had made the attack on us, we thought we would give
them a chance to fight in close quarters if they wanted
to do so. On account of their superior numbers—they
now had over two hundred — we expected them to
close in on us in a final charge. We were well prepared
to meet such an emergency.

Had we known what our friends were doing at that
moment, which will be mentioned later, we would have
broken through their lines and gone out if there had
been double the number there really was. Firing continued from both sides through the night, about the
same as the night before.

During the night we could hear men working with
axes, saws, and hammers behind a hill about three hundred and fifty or four hundred yards west of our

trenches. At one time we heard a loud explosion where
the rustlers were working that sounded like the bursting of a shell or bomb. We soon 'called the turn' which
we afterwards found to be correct. They had taken a
wagon back of this hill, well out of sight of our sharp-
shooters in the trenches, and also a supply of timber,
and constructed what they called a 'go devil,' made
on somewhat the same plan as our outfit that we used in
burning the K C Ranch, except that they had a platform that about sixteen men could stand on behind
upright posts for breastworks, with a team of horses
hitched on the end of a long tongue, with the heads of
the team in the direction that they wanted to travel.
A driver could get behind the team hitched to the end
of the tongue and push the two-wheel 'go devil' anywhere he wanted to go. Sixteen men could stand on the
platform and still be behind the breastworks in front of
them. It must have been an ingenious construction.
I understand it was invented by Arapaho Brown and
built under his instructions and that he had a lot of
bombs manufactured by himself and a good supply of
dynamite with fuse attachment. The plan was to push
this outfit up to us, then throw the bombs and dynamite into our trenches. We expected this and prepared for it. I was in the trenches myself all that night
with fifteen men. We dug a trench through the soft
sand extending from the bottom of our old trench in a
westerly direction towards the enemy. This trench
ran along the edge of a bluff and was about fifty feet
long and deep enough to conceal fifteen or twenty men.

In driving their machine up to a point near enough to throw dynamite or bombs into our rifle pits, they would have to pass the new trench where we were concealed and could get in there from no other direction. We would then have them in the open and at close quarters. After we had finished this job we gathered tumble weeds and dry sagebrush in a few feet of us and covered up the new trench so completely that it could not be seen even in daylight. Then we waited all developments.

A short time after sunrise next morning the 'go devil' came plainly in sight and for some reason stopped on top of the hill from behind which they had been working the night before. The black flag was nailed to the top of a post from one side and a red flag on the other side. The black flag meant 'no quarter' and as the inventor of the machine was an anarchist I presume the red colors represented his principles. Dave Booker, who was on his knees with his 45–70 Winchester at one end of our trenches, had been watching every movement of the 'go devil,' and when it stopped on the hill three shots rang out in rapid succession from our rifle pits, and each shot could be heard plainly to strike their breastworks. Booker had become anxious to send them a challenge and could not resist the temptation to take a shot. His action probably saved the lives of several men, but it was a great disappointment to every man in the trenches and he was severely censured for it. In a few minutes the rustlers had drawn the machine from sight and never

attempted to show up with it any more. This was the
third day of the siege at the $\bar{\Lambda}$ ranch.

About noon a column of mounted troops of the
United States Army could be seen marching from the
direction of Fort McKinney and coming towards the
ranch. They marched the troops up to a point about
eight hundred yards from our trenches and formed them
behind a hill. All firing from both sides had ceased.
The commanding officer of the United States forces
then rode out with ten or twelve of his staff and raised
the white flag. I directed one of our men to tie a white
handkerchief on the end of his rifle and raise it up over
our breastworks. The officer then approached and
came up to our trenches. The commanding officer informed me that he had been ordered by the President
of the United States to arrest all parties on the ground
engaged in this combat and to restore order. I told him
that Major Wolcott, who was at the ranchhouse at
that time, was in command of our party, but that I
could answer for myself and the fifteen men in the
trenches, which was that we would surrender to the
military authorities provided he would arrest this mob
who had been firing on us for three days and nights.
Major Wolcott then approached from the house and
held a conference with the commanding officer and I
think repeated about what I had told him myself. The
officer promised to arrest the leaders of the attacking
parties if it were possible for him to do so. We then
surrendered to the military authorities with the under-
standing that we deliver our rifles but retain our side

arms. Leaders of the rustlers had all disappeared and I do not think any of them were arrested at that time.

We found that there were many people out there with the rustlers who were our friends, and who were very much surprised to meet us and to find who was in our party. We all lined up and proceeded to Fort McKinney with the troops, where we were allowed the courtesy of the limits of the posts. Two of our men who had been badly wounded at the Ⱶ ranch were placed in the hospital at Fort McKinney. Both of them died. Upon meeting our friends who came up to Buffalo to see us, we learned that during the fight at the Ⱶ ranch the rustlers had circulated the report all over the country that they had us overpowered and so completely hemmed in that it was only a matter of hours until they would have us all killed. Our friends in Buffalo and Cheyenne, Wyoming, then got busy, and believing that they were doing the only thing to save our lives, wired President Harrison, who was at that time chief executive, to send troops out of Fort McKinney for our relief. Of course, the military authorities could only act in a way to restore order and were supposed to do this by arresting the parties engaged in the fight. But after the arrest was made it meant a trial in the civil courts. We all knew that our friends thought they had done what was best for us, but they made a very serious mistake, which resulted in the ruin of many of us financially and completely broke up all our plans for the campaign against the rustlers.

Complaint having been filed against us in Johnson

County by the criminal element, we demanded a trial at once. But the prosecuting attorney of Johnson County found that it would be impossible to secure a jury, as the people were lined up to a man on one side or the other. The lawyers on both sides agreed to a change of venue to Cheyenne, the capital of the Territory. We were then conducted by the troops to Cheyenne and turned over to Major Egbert, commanding officer of Fort Russell, which is just outside the limits of Cheyenne. Major Egbert treated us as honored guests and extended to us every courtesy possible. Judge Willis Vandevanter of Cheyenne was leading lawyer in our case.

Jack Flag had started a rustler paper in Buffalo in which he wrote a series of stories denouncing the cattlemen and all of our party as murderers of the most vicious type. The 'Rocky Mountain News' at Denver printed all these malicious reports in red headlines on the front page of that paper. As it was near the time for general election in Wyoming some of the other papers over the Territory took up the cry of the rustlers and assailed our party for the purpose of making political capital out of it, as they were strongly opposed to several members of our party who were prominent in politics. But they went too strong and could not sustain any of their slanderous charges, and a reaction in public sentiment among men who had formerly sympathized with the rustlers was the result.

The rustlers in Johnson County were getting worse. They murdered George Wellman, who was foreman of the Hoe Ranch, owned by Henry A. Blair of Chicago, on the road between Powder River and Buffalo. Wellman was a young man of excellent character, loved by every one who knew him, and a prominent member of the Masonic Lodge. This cowardly murder by the rustlers after we left Fort McKinney had turned what few sympathizers they had among the settlers against them.

We were indicted upon our own request in the courts of Cheyenne and our trial commenced. This was the most famous case ever brought to trial in the Northwest, and lasted for more than a month.

When the prosecuting attorney had examined five hundred jurors and failed to secure twelve men who were qualified to serve, he submitted a motion to dismiss the case. Our lawyer strenuously objected to this motion, stating to the court that his clients demanded an immediate trial and were ready to fight this case in open court, the same as they had fought the rustlers in the open in Johnson County, and that he would not agree to anything except a verdict from the jury. The court then issued an order for eight hundred more jurors. After more than one thousand had been examined, a jury was secured and then proceeded with the trial, which did not last long after they got into the case. The jury, without leaving their seats, returned a verdict of 'not guilty' on every count and in each case.

We were fully exonerated from the charges by a jury of *bona-fide* citizens and were free men. Public opinion was strongly in our favor now, all over the territory.

The rustlers had commenced stealing stock from the settlers in Johnson County and martial law had been declared. United States troops were sent into the county and stationed at Gillette and on Lower Powder River. Most of the rustlers left the country.

Arapaho Brown organized a small band of thieves on Powder River but he 'double-crossed' some of them, and his own men murdered him in a lone cabin in the woods and burned his body to cinders. This was a just retribution for the vicious life that the man had lived.

It has never been any trouble since to convict a cattle thief in Johnson County. We made it safe for an honest man to live in that county and enjoy the fruits of his labor, but it cost our party one hundred thousand dollars to accomplish this. Some of them were able financially to stand it. But when I had paid my *pro rata* of the expenses I had nothing left.

CHAPTER V

OKLAHOMA OUTLAWS

In the early part of 1893 my old friend Mr. P. B. Weare, of Chicago, who owned a large cattle ranch in Montana, and the Honorable J. Sterling Morton, of Nebraska City, Nebraska, offered me a position as superintendent of the Nebraska City Packing Company located at Nebraska City.

I accepted this position and moved to Nebraska City with my family. This splendid old-fashioned city on the banks of the Missouri River was so quiet, and the business that I was engaged in so different from the active life that I had lived for so many years in the West, that it soon became monotonous, and after about a year's service I sent in my resignation, with a view of hunting a new field in which to operate, where I would have more active work and some excitement.

The Indian Territory had been a rendezvous for the worst gang of outlaws in the Southwest for many years. Oklahoma proper was opened for settlement in 1889; later in 1893 what was known as the Cherokee Strip was thrown open for settlement, also as a part of Oklahoma.

The opening of Oklahoma for settlers brought many thousands of good men and women to the country who were honest in wanting to secure land and built up homes for themselves, but it brought also many fugitives from justice who had been driven out of other States. Some of the worst outlaws in Montana who had been driven out by Granville Stuart in 1879 were in the run for claims in Oklahoma. They were there from Texas, Kansas, Arkansas, and many other States, ready for the run for claims when the signal to start was given by the United States officer.

There was no discrimination nor favoritism. The man who had the best horse and knew how to ride him generally got the best claim.

I went to Oklahoma in the spring of 1894. I sent for my wife and daughter and located at Pawnee, Oklahoma. I accepted the position with Frank Lake as undersheriff of Pawnee County. I was also appointed United States Deputy Marshal of Oklahoma by E. D. Nix, who was Chief Marshal with headquarters at Guthrie, the capital. I was also appointed United States Deputy by Mr. George Crump, who was at that time United States Marshal of the western district of Arkansas with headquarters at Fort Smith, and had charge of the Federal Court under Judge Parker.

For many years this was the largest criminal court in the world. The records show that during the administration of Judge Parker, which lasted about twenty years, he sentenced more murderers to death than any other judge in America. However, this was not strange considering the class of criminals he had to deal with. Before the opening of Oklahoma to settlement, his jurisdiction took in all of the Indian Territory and the western district of Arkansas.

Judge Parker was really a just and kind-hearted man, but he was never known to shirk his duty under the law.

Having received all the authority that I needed as an officer with jurisdiction extending over all of the Indian Territory and Oklahoma, I began to lay my plans to break up the organized bands of outlaws, who had been robbing trains, banks, stores, committing murder, and in fact openly defying the law for years.

The most notorious gang in Oklahoma at that time was the Daltons, including Bob, Bill, Emmett, and Grat Dalton, brothers, Bill Doolin, Bitter Creek (George Newcomb), Charley Pierce, Red Buck (Buck Weightman), Tulsa Jack, Bill Raidler, Diamond Dick, and others. These men were all noted outlaws with large rewards offered for their capture, dead or alive. This gang had a rendezvous near Ingalls, Oklahoma, just over the line in Payne County about twenty miles south of Pawnee, which they used as a base for their operations when returning from a raid on some bank or railroad train in Texas, Arkansas, Kansas, or Missouri.

Up to this time there had never been one of this Dalton gang killed or captured in Oklahoma, although the United States Government had authorized the Marshal of Oklahoma to appoint a large number of Special United States Deputies and possemen to hunt down the bandits.

At one time there were more than a hundred Deputy Marshals and possemen in Oklahoma under United States Marshal Nix. The first 'knock-out blow' ever received by the Dalton gang was given them by the citizens of Coffeeville, Kansas, in 1892. The bandits attempted to rob two banks in the town in broad daylight. The result was that Bob Dalton, Grat Dalton, Bill Farius, and Dick Broadwell were killed, and Emmett Dalton, the youngest brother, was wounded and captured. He finally recovered and was sentenced to the penitentiary for life. Later he was paroled or pardoned. This left Bill Dalton, leader of the gang, Buck Weightman (alias Red Buck), Bill Doolin, Tulsa Jack, Charley Pierce, Bill Raidler, George Raidler, George Newcomb (alias Bitter Creek, alias the Slaughter Kid).

In addition to the regular outlaws whose names I have mentioned, there were also about twenty-five or thirty members of this gang scattered about over Pawnee and Payne Counties, who worked under cover, and acted as a 'fence' for the wild bunch in disposing of stolen cattle and horses, and giving information to the active members of the gang relative to the movement of the officers.

The most prominent and dangerous of this class were the Dunn boys, and James brothers, who had secured claims near each other located about twenty miles south and east of Pawnee near Ingalls. Their home was a rendezvous for the Dalton gang when they were in the country.

THE DALTON BROTHERS AND THEIR SISTER

Bill Dunn appeared to be the leader of the Dunn brothers. He was a dead shot, and I think he was the quickest man with a revolver that I ever met. He and Chris Bolton owned a meat market in Pawnee, Oklahoma, where they disposed of stolen cattle. Sheriff Lake and I had arrested them several times for stealing cattle, but they always managed to give bond. Chris Bolton attended to the butcher shop while Bill Dunn rode the range and furnished the stolen beef.

Finally we received sufficient evidence against Chris Bolton to send him to the 'pen' for cattle stealing. This conviction caused the Dunn boys to become very uneasy and restless. They soon made a proposition to Sheriff Lake and myself that if we would not prosecute them, they would furnish us information that would surely lead to the capture of the leaders of the Dalton gang.

I had felt for some time that if we could ever get the Dunn boys to furnish this information we would have the key to the situation, and in a short time could break up the Dalton gang entirely.

Sheriff Lake and I then arranged for a conference with Bill Dunn and one of his brothers in Pawnee. At this conference we gave the Dunn boys to understand plainly that we knew they were members of the Dalton gang and had committed many crimes with other members of the gang, but that so far as we were personally concerned, we would not prosecute them any further and would use our influence with United States Marshal Nix to have him promise the same thing, provided, however, that they would sign an agreement to the following effect:

> That they would sever all relations with the Daltons, Doolin, and other outlaws, obey the laws of the country and make good citizens, and provided further, that the first time any of the Dalton gang came into that part of the country, the Dunn boys should immediately bring word to Sheriff Lake and myself of their exact location.

We did not ask them to assist us in the capture, nor did we expect them to do so. All that we exacted of them was positive information as to the time of the arrival of the outlaws, and the place they were stopping.

We also agreed with the Dunns that, in the event that we captured any or all of the outlaws, we would have United States Marshal Nix collect the rewards offered for their capture, and turn the money all over to the Dunn boys, with the exception of a sufficient amount to be paid to Sheriff Lake and myself to cover our actual expenses while hunting the outlaws. At that time there was from one to three thousand dollars offered for the body of each of the 'wild bunch,' dead or alive.

The Dunn boys willingly agreed to our terms, provided that United States Marshal Nix would also sign this agreement. We then took the two Dunn boys to Guthrie and held a conference with Marshal Nix in his office. We outlined the proposition to him, and he agreed to all the terms of the agreement. Then he had a regular contract drawn up, which was signed by all of us, including Marshal Nix, and each man retained a copy of same.

The Dunns then returned to their homes, after promising Sheriff Lake and me that they would report to us at Pawnee from time to time.

I told Marshal Nix that since Sheriff Lake and I were undertaking a very dangerous and hazardous job, I wanted his promise of absolute secrecy and that no other officer on his force should be advised of our plans. He promised me that my wishes would be carried out absolutely, and said that he wanted to turn the entire matter over to me.

Sheriff Lake and I then returned to Pawnee and commenced to lay our plans for the work ahead of us. The Dalton gang and especially Bill Doolin had many friends among the settlers south of Pawnee along the Cimarron River, and along the line of Pawnee County. There is no doubt that Doolin furnished many of them money to buy groceries to live upon when they first settled in that country and had a hard struggle for existence. They appreciated his kindness even though he was an outlaw with a price on his head, and there were plenty of people who would get up at the hour of midnight if necessary to ride to Bill Doolin to warn him of the approach of officers when they were seen in that vicinity. For this reason it was almost impossible for a party of officers to travel together through that country without being seen by some friend of the outlaws, who would always give the alarm in time for the criminals to escape.

For this reason Sheriff Lake and I decided not to take a posse of deputies into that country, but to undertake the capture alone. Our plan was to make a still hunt, work under cover, and depend upon the Dunn boys to let us know when the outlaws were in the country. We got a mess outfit and a good supply of ammunition and made a night ride to the Dunn settlement. We made a camp in the hills where there was heavy timber and water, near the outlaw rendezvous. Then we notified the Dunns and took them out to our camp. We told them that we expected to remain under cover until they reported to us that the outlaws were in the country, and that all we asked of them was to furnish us information promptly as to when the outlaws dropped in, and that if we moved our camp we would always let them know our exact location. They said they were certain the outlaws would come to their place, but that they could not tell just how long it would be. They said that the gang at that time was scattered, that Bill Doolin had not been seen for several weeks, that his wife lived at a store and post office called Lawson, some eight miles north of Dal Dunn's place. They also said that Bill Doolin for several months had been talking seriously of giving himself up to us and Marshal Nix, provided he could get a promise of some clemency. They said that Red Buck, Bitter Creek, and Charley Pierce were now riding together and that these three were likely to drop in at any time, for they said that they owed Bitter Creek one thousand dollars and he would come in to get his money if for no other reason. They again assured us before leaving that they would carry out their part of the contract.

We now realized that it was a waiting game. We also knew that we were taking our lives into our hands, for we knew that the Dunn boys had no love for us, and that it would be an easy matter for them to lead us into a trap where we would not even have a fighting chance for our lives. But we figured that they would not play the game that way, because if they had us killed, we knew that there would be no money in it for them, and that every officer in the territory would be in the field hunting them down. On the other hand, if they played fair with us, and we succeeded in the capture, they would get a good reward, so we decided that under the circumstances they would do what they had promised.

Nothing happened to break the monotony for about a week. The Dunns then reported that the Rock Island train had been held up and robbed by the Dalton gang, at Dover, Oklahoma, and that they were looking for the gang to show up at the rendezvous at any time, to get fresh horses and rest up a few days as they usually did.

The names of the robbers who participated in this hold-up were Tulsa Jack, Bitter Creek, Red Buck, and Charley Pierce. Chris Madsen, Deputy United States Marshal for Oklahoma, had charge of the district at Pond Creek at that time. After the robbery a posse of Deputy Marshals from Pond Creek followed the trail of the bandits out into the hills and surprised them in a canyon. In the fight that followed Tulsa Jack was killed. The other three made their escape.

We now expected a report at any time that the outlaws were in the neighborhood. We kept a close watch and remained in camp for several days. One evening we rode over to George McElroy's ranch, six or eight miles from the Dunn place. We notified the Dunn boys where they would find us in case we were needed, and that we expected to stay all night at McElroy's. We fed our saddle horses and cared for them for the night. The next morning we found that our horses had broken out of the corral during the night and left us afoot. We struck their trail, but had a long tramp before we found them. We saw one of the Dunn boys that day, and he told us that the night we stopped at McElroy's ranch three of the gang, Pierce, Bitter Creek, and Red Buck had come to their place and stopped all night, and had left early the next morning. The Dunns said that they hunted for us to report, but could not find us. Whether this was true or not we never knew. The next we heard of the outlaws they were on the Verdigris River in the Cherokee country.

As Sheriff Lake was compelled to return to Pawnee to attend to some business at the office, we came back together. We still kept in touch with the Dunn boys and depended upon them for information as to where the outlaws were.

There was a very troublesome character by the name of Lon McCool, who owned a feed stable in Pawnee.

He was a receiver of stolen property. His business was to handle horses stolen in Texas, Kansas, and Arkansas by the different bands of horse thieves, wherever he could find a market for them. He was an open enemy of the officers of the county, and was especially bitter against me. He never lost an opportunity to warn a criminal if he thought I was hunting him.

One day I received a description of a man wanted for murder in Kansas, with an order from the sheriff for his arrest. I arrested on suspicion a fellow whom I believed to be the right man, and put him in jail, and then notified the sheriff. The next day I had occasion to go to Cleveland, thirty miles east of Pawnee, on important business. I made the ride horseback and returned about dusk. I found that during the day lawyers had managed to have the prisoner released under *habeas corpus*. I also found a telegram from the sheriff in Kansas saying 'Hold the prisoner at all hazards. I am on my way.'

Immediately I sent out for George Hanner, one of the gamest deputies on the sheriff's force. George told me that he had been watching the accused man, since he was released, and that he was now in Lon McCool's bunkhouse. I had taken off my six-shooter and laid my Winchester aside when I first rode in. I had a heavy pocket derringer that I usually carried in my hip pocket when in town. It was a forty-one-caliber Colt. I thought it was a good one, but had never tried it out.

We found our man in McCool's bunkhouse. After we had arrested and handcuffed him, I took a seat on a keg and began reading the telegram to the prisoner, when Lon McCool walked into the shack. When he saw me he asked in a very insulting and abusive way what I was doing in his house. I told him that I had a habit of going wherever I pleased, and at the present time I had a prisoner there in my custody. My reply appeared to make him furious. He stepped up close in front of me, and with his left hand slapped me in the face, at the same time dropping his right hand to his hip pocket. In rising from the keg on which I was seated, I pushed him away from me, and at the same time drew my derringer and fired at his head. The bullet struck him in the forehead just over the left eye. He fell on his back, and I supposed from the appearance of the wound that he was shot square through the head.

I then sent out for a doctor, who came over at once, and with the assistance of Deputy United States Marshal Joe Eads, we put the body on a blanket and carried it to McCool's home near by. I put the prisoner in jail and held him until the sheriff from Kansas arrived. He identified the prisoner as the man he wanted. He took him to Winfield, Kansas, where he was sentenced to life imprisonment for murder.

When the doctor examined the wound in Lon Mc-Cool's head, he found that the bullet had not penetrated his head, but had glanced around the skull under the skin, and come out at the back of his head. He was unconscious for twelve hours, then commenced to improve. I believe he would have finally recovered had he taken good care of himself, but after he got up and commenced feeling better, he started in to beat up a Dutch boy, and got the worst of it very badly. He died in about a month at Pawnee. I threw away this derringer that I had, and have never carried one since.

Sheriff Lake and I were still on the lookout for the Dalton gang, and expected to get some of them at least through the Dunn boys.

One morning I received a telegram from the United States Marshal's office at Guthrie, saying, 'Come down at once, the Dunn boys have just brought in the dead bodies of two of the Dalton gang.'

Sheriff Lake and I immediately went to Guthrie. We found Dal Dunn and John at Guthrie, and the dead bodies of Charley Pierce and Bitter Creek (George Newcomb). Pierce had been killed with a shotgun loaded with buckshot, and had several bad wounds in his body, and was shot in the bottom of the feet with buckshot, which proved that he must have been shot while lying down.

It was the general opinion that they were shot while asleep. The body of Pierce was badly swollen. He appeared to have been dead for some time, but the body of Bitter Creek looked perfectly natural, and looked as though he had not been dead very long.

The story that Dal Dunn told to John Hale, Chief Deputy United States Marshal at Guthrie, was that Bitter Creek and Charley Pierce came to Dal Dunn's place the night before, and that Bill, Dal, and John Dunn were there waiting for them. When the outlaws dismounted and came into the yard, the Dunn boys shot them down. Bitter Creek was shot in the arm and also in the head, and they supposed that he was shot square through the head. The Dunn boys then hitched up a team to a wagon, spread out a tarpaulin, in the bottom of the wagon bed, put the bodies of the outlaws in the wagon with all their guns, and covered them up. Then Dal and John Dunn started to drive the outfit across the country to Guthrie to deliver the dead bodies and claim the reward. Bill Dunn remained at the rendezvous to obliterate all trace of the blood in the yard where the outlaws were shot down. During that day Bill Tighlman and Heck Thomas, two Deputy United States Marshals, rode up to Dunn's place with a posse of men. When they learned that Bitter Creek and Pierce had been killed, and their bodies taken to Guthrie, they all came in.

When Dal Dunn and John were driving across the country at night with the bodies of the outlaws, some-where between Stillwater and Guthrie, they noticed that the tarpaulin under which the bodies lay was moving. Dal raised the canvas and found that Bitter Creek was alive, and was trying to put a cartridge into a revolver that he held in his hand. The outlaw begged Dunn for 'God's sake to spare his life.' As they were just passing a house at the side of the road Dunn did not care to raise an alarm, but struck Bitter Creek a blow with his revolver, and knocked him senseless. As soon as they passed the house Dal Dunn shot the outlaw through the head.

I presume that accounts for the fact that the body of Bitter Creek was not swollen and looked natural when they brought the bodies into Guthrie. It appears that when the outlaws were first shot at Dunn's place a bullet struck Bitter Creek in the side of the head and glanced off. It made a bloody wound and the Dunn boys thought he was dead. It must have been an awful awakening to him when he regained consciousness and found himself soaked in the blood of his dead partner who was lying by his side in the wagon bed.

There was a reward of a thousand dollars offered by the Rock Island Railroad Company for the capture of Charley Pierce for the hold-up of their train at Dover, Oklahoma, and I think the Santa Fé Company offered fifteen hundred dollars for the capture of Bitter Creek for robbing the Santa Fé at Red Rock, Oklahoma. These rewards were paid.

Sheriff Lake and I decided that we would have nothing more to do with the Dunn boys, as we had no confidence in their promise to reform and make good citizens, and so I notified United States Marshal Nix.

There were two brothers by the name of Bill and John Shelley who lived in the eastern part of Pawnee County near the Arkansas River. One of them had a young woman with him, whom he claimed was his wife. They were both dead hard men, but did not appear to belong to any particular gang of outlaws. The two brothers were always together. They stole saddles, harness, horses, or anything that they could sell for a dollar. We got a strong case against them, arrested them, and locked them up in jail at Pawnee. We held them in jail for some time waiting for court to convene.

In the mean time, Mrs. Shelley would often visit the jail to see them. She was always searched by a woman under the sheriff's direction before she was permitted to enter the jail. One day she visited the jail earlier than usual, and in some way succeeded in slipping a loaded revolver to the Shelleys. That evening the jailer opened the cell door to hand the prisoners a bucket of water. He was immediately held up at the point of a revolver, pulled into the cell, gagged, and his revolver and ammunition taken from him. The prisoners then walked out and under the cover of darkness stole two of the best horses in town and made their escape.

The woman returned to their cabin in the woods and remained there alone for some time. She had a large, black Newfoundland dog that was a beautiful specimen. His name was 'Bum,' and he was very much attached to the woman. We watched this cabin for a long time, but in spite of our vigilance the woman and dog gave us the slip and left the country. We knew she would go to the Shelleys, but we never did find out how she got out of that country, nor the direction she had taken.

We were particularly anxious to recapture the Shelley brothers, for we found that they were wanted for several vicious murders in other States.

After several months Cook Horton of Pawnee, who

at that time was a special deputy under Sheriff Lake, was making a trip to Tulsa in a one-horse buggy. He had a young man from Arkansas in the buggy with him. They met the two Shelleys in the road in a deep bottom along the Arkansas River. Horton recognized them at once and opened fire on them with his revolver at close range. The outlaws returned the fire, then dashed into the heavy timber on their horses, and escaped. Cook Horton reported to us that he was sure that he shot one of them in the face.

Finally we located the outlaws in a cabin in the heavy woods eight miles east of Checotah in the Creek Nation by first getting track of the woman and Newfoundland dog. Sheriff Lake got a wagon and team, a good camp outfit, and a party of us started on the hunt for the outlaws. This was in the winter of 1895, and I remember we had the heaviest snowstorm that I have ever seen in the Southwest. We started out in a snowstorm, and it continued for three days. When we reached Tulsa, we were joined by Dr. Bland, who would always get up at midnight if necessary to hunt a horse thief, and Dean Hogan, a Deputy United States Marshal. When we reached Checotah I hunted up John McCann, who had seen long service as a Deputy United States Marshal in the Indian Territory, and as he knew where the cabin was located, I asked him to lead our party out to the rendezvous. He consented willingly to do so. I think there were six of us in the party, and every man had a big supply of ammunition. We reached the cabin some two hours before daylight.

Sheriff Lake's plan was for us all to get up close to the cabin and wait until daylight. Then Sheriff Lake would call in to the outlaws, and he thought that they would come out and surrender when they found that we had the cabin surrounded. I did not agree with the sheriff on this plan, for I did not believe these men would surrender under any consideration unless we had the dead drop on them. I proposed that each of us select a position under cover where we could watch the two doors, and wait quietly until they came out, then hold them up at the point of our guns, which might save some of our men from getting hurt. Sheriff Lake did not like my plan, for he said he wanted to take them alive, and thought probably some one might fire and kill them as they came out of the door. I told him all right, I could stand it if he could.

We had already examined the small barn twenty-five yards north of the cabin, and found four horses and two saddles, so we felt sure that the two men were in the cabin. The house was built of logs with 'chinking' (sticks between the logs plastered with mud), about twelve by twelve feet, a door in the north, and one in the south. There were no windows. The cabin was in an open space in the woods. No underbrush was near, but plenty of big trees all about for several hundred yards. We took our position around the cabin and were all up close to it, and waited until daylight. The ground was covered with heavy snow and it was awfully cold.

Just as daylight was breaking good, Sheriff Lake

shouted 'Hello.' A voice from within immediately answered 'Hello.' Sheriff Lake recognized his voice, and then told Shelley who he was and what his business was there, and told him to come out and surrender. Shelley answered very coolly, and said, 'All right, we will be out as soon as we can dress.' We could then hear them moving about on the inside of the cabin, making a noise like dragging something over the floor, or moving furniture. This lasted for several minutes, then everything was deathly quiet.

I had taken a position on the east side of the south door, and placed John McCann on the west side, but we were standing on each side within a few feet of the cabin, not directly in front of the door, but with magazine Winchesters, caliber 38–56, in our hands ready for action. We had not heard a sound for about ten minutes. The suspense was very unpleasant, and I thought that it was time for a change. I called in to the outlaws and asked, 'Do you intend to surrender or not?' Their answer was, 'No, damn you! If you want us, come in and get us.' Then I asked Shelley if his wife was with him. He answered that she was. I told him to send her out, that we would not hurt her. The door near us was then opened just wide enough for one person to pass out. The woman stepped out under our guns, followed by the Newfoundland dog. The door was pulled shut immediately and fastened from within. I asked the woman how many men were in the cabin.

She answered, 'No one but John and Bill Shelley.'

When I stepped up close to the woman to ask these

questions the black dog gave a low growl and showed his white fangs. He had a glitter in his eyes that did not look good to me, but when I spoke kindly and called him 'Bum,' he came up and licked my hand. I told the woman to leave us and not to come back. She disappeared in the woods, her dog following her. Then I called in again and asked the Shelleys to surrender. They told me to go to H——. In less than three minutes a shot was fired from the inside through a hole between the logs just in front of McCann. He dropped to his knees, but immediately raised himself up on his feet, staggering as he did so. I asked him in a low tone of voice if he were badly hurt. He placed his right hand over his heart and said he would be all right in a few minutes.

The bullet had hit him directly over the heart, but had struck his forty-five Colt's revolver that he carried in a shoulder scabbard and glanced off. It was a close call.

Then I motioned to McCann to get ready to cross-fire on the door. We emptied our magazines into the door in quick succession from each side. During this rapid fire we heard distinctly a noise from the inside that sounded like some one kicking or scrambling on the floor. We concluded that one of them was hit.

A few moments later Dr. Bland changed his position to the north side and was just raising his gun to fire through the north door, when another shot was fired from within. This struck the doctor in the arm and made a very painful, but not serious wound.

The outlaws kept firing from the inside of the cabin. They would take out the 'chinking' from between the logs, and make a porthole from which to fire. They could see us plainly, but we could not see them. Then I suggested to Sheriff Lake that we fall back from the cabin and get under cover where we could cross-fire into the cabin at close range and shoot through their portholes. He approved of this move. We all took positions completely surrounding the cabin from twenty-five to thirty yards away. I selected a position at the small house twenty-five yards north of the cabin.

We kept up a steady cross-fire from every direction until about 3 P.M., shooting into every crack or hole in the walls and doors. Our shots were always answered by the outlaws whom I still thought were unhurt and determined to fight to the last. I had expected to see them make a dash for liberty, and we were all prepared for this move. As it was getting late in the afternoon, I decided that the outlaws intended to 'stand us off' until night if possible, then to escape in the darkness.

I called Sheriff Lake over to me and told him that if he and his men would hold their positions and keep a close watch on the cabin, I would devise a plan to drive the outlaws from the cabin.

I mounted my horse and galloped over to a farmer's house about a mile away. I met the farmer as he was driving in with a load of hay. Without any ceremony I directed him to drive his wagon and hay down to the cabin, and explained to him that I would probably want to burn up the wagon and hay in order to run the outlaws out in the open. In that event I would pay him his price for his wagon and hay. Also I got an axe, saw, and a five-gallon can of coal oil that he had bought in Checotah the day before.

We drove this outfit down near the barn under a little hill where we were protected from the bullets of the outlaws. We unloaded the hay, uncoupled the wagon, fastened the coupling pole solid to the rear axle-tree, then we got seasoned oak fence-rails and lashed them on to the hind axletree in an upright position with our picket ropes. The bottom of the rails was about two feet from the ground, the top extended two feet above a man's head. Then we used a large bundle of the dry hay tied up by ropes in front of the rails. This was drawn up so that it would not rest on the ground. Then we saturated the hay with coal oil and fastened the coal-oil can on so that the rest of the oil could be used when the 'go devil' was pushed up against the cabin.

This was the same kind of an outfit that I had used in Wyoming during the rustler war, when we had the fight at the K C Ranch on Powder River.

We selected two men who walked behind the breast-works and pushed the outfit up against the cabin. The outlaws fired on the two men, but did no damage. While this was going on the rest of us were pouring lead into the portholes as fast as we could shoot. When the two men reached the cabin they stood behind the breastworks, and with a small bucket they threw coal oil all over the cabin, cut the ropes to let the hay down against the wall, pulled the wagon back, struck a match, and set the hay on fire. In an instant the cabin was in flames.

The outlaws saw now that they were doomed. It was either surrender, or a worse fate. They called out at the top of their voices that they would surrender.

They were ordered to come out with their hands up and leave their guns on the inside. At the same time the order was given to the men not to fire on them. Then the two outlaws came out with their hands up. At this moment the Shelley woman came running in from the woods, screaming for us not to shoot the outlaws.

We all closed in about the prisoners and searched them, but found that they had left their guns inside. In searching John Shelley I found that each of his boots was nearly half full of blood. He said he was shot early in the game, when McCann and I first cross-fired on the door. Shelley said that when he was hit he was squatted down on the floor just taking aim at one of us through a porthole. He was shot through both thighs, the ball lodging in his right hip. I could see now why they did not make a dash for liberty. John was not able to run, and his brother would not leave him. Just how any man could stand on his feet and fight all day with such bad wounds is more than I can understand, but he collapsed absolutely when it was all over. His brother never had a scratch, although several bullets had passed through his clothes.

When the coal oil burned off the cabin the blaze died down, and as there was plenty of snow, we all set to work throwing snow balls on the fire and finally put it out.

The inside of this cabin was a curiosity. Dirt and splinters were scattered all over the room. There was hardly a square inch on the inside that had not been struck by bullets. We had burned up nearly eight hundred rounds of ammunition during the day.

I think we found four Winchesters, several revolvers, and one very fine shotgun, and plenty of ammunition in the house. Also four new saddles under the beds. There was a very large Saratoga trunk up against the north door, which was full of men's suits that had never been worn, and women's nice clothes. But the trunk had about fifty bullet holes in it, and I think the clothes were shot to pieces. There were also four stolen horses in the stable. We noticed a scar on the face of one of the men, which he said was from the revolver shot that Cook Horton gave him when they met in the trail on the Arkansas River.

In all my experience I have never known outlaws to pull off a gamer fight than the Shelley brothers.

We had to send to Checotah for an ambulance and stretcher in order to handle the wounded prisoner. We told the Shelley woman that we would take the prisoners to Fort Smith, Arkansas, for trial. She said she would have to stay at home until she disposed of some property they had. I could not help but pity the woman. She was young and rather good-looking. No doubt her early training had forced her to lead such a life. We left her alone in the cabin with her faithful friend 'Bum.'

We took the prisoners to Fort Smith and they were tried in Judge Parker's court, and I think sentenced to eight years for resisting officers and assault with intent to murder.

About this time the notorious Cherokee Bill was captured and sentenced to death for murder. He was in jail at Fort Smith awaiting the death sentence to be carried out. Later on the Shelley woman came to Fort Smith to see them. The Shelley boys induced her to bring them a loaded revolver as they did in Pawnee. Shelley then managed to slip this revolver to Cherokee Bill, who was locked up in his cell. Then Bill sent for the head jailer, Larry Keating. While the jailer stood in front of the jail door, Cherokee Bill covered him with the revolver and ordered him to unlock the door. Keating refused to comply with the demand and Cherokee Bill shot him dead, although his cell was locked, and he knew he could not get out.

Cherokee Bill was executed a short time after this.

CHAPTER VI

THE END OF THE 'WILD BUNCH'

BILL DOOLIN had left the rest of the outlaw gang and had been keeping very quiet for some time. It was currently rumored that he intended to give himself up. I am sure there were some good men in Oklahoma who would have been pleased to see Doolin stand trial, and come clear if it were possible for him to do so.

Later it was reported that Deputy United States Marshal Bill Tilghman had captured Bill Doolin at Eureka Springs, Arkansas. I was in Guthrie when Tilghman brought Doolin in. The prisoner was not handcuffed nor shackled. He was allowed utmost freedom about the jail, and appeared to be perfectly contented.

Soon after Bill Doolin was placed in jail, United States Marshal Nix retired from office, and P. S. Nagle, of Kingfisher, Oklahoma, was appointed in his place. I was offered a commission as a deputy under Mr. Nagle, and as I had a lot of official business to finish up in Oklahoma, I accepted it.

It was generally believed among officers of the Territory that Dynamite Dick had been shot and killed in the hills between Cleveland, Oklahoma, and Tulsa, and that his body had not been identified, but I had reliable information that he was in Arizona, and was 'very much alive.' However, before I could get out there he had murdered and robbed two Mexicans on a sheep ranch and disappeared. Next I located him near Smith Paul's Valley, in the Chickasaw Nation. His correct name was Dan Clifton, and his mother lived near Paul's Valley.

I selected Clarence Young, one of the gamest Deputy Marshals in Oklahoma, who knew Dynamite Dick by sight, to go with me. Before we got into that country, a posse of Deputy Marshals from Paris, Texas, had got the drop on Dynamite, and arrested him. They found a bottle of whiskey in his pocket, and as they had no idea who he was, and had no other charge against him, they took him before the nearest United States Commissioner, and he was sentenced to jail for thirty days for introducing whiskey into an Indian country. The deputies took him to Paris, Texas, and were paid seventy-five cents for the arrest, and mileage for taking him down. There was a reward of twenty-five hundred dollars on Dynamite, dead or alive. When his thirty days were up I went to Paris, Texas, and met Shep Williams, Marshal of that district, produced a warrant from Oklahoma for murder in the first degree against Dan Clifton, and demanded the prisoner. When I went to the jail to identify him, Dick had on a very high standing collar, a derby hat, and about four weeks' growth of stubby beard on his face. I sent for a barber and had him shaved, although he protested against this, for he knew what I was looking for. When the hair was shaved off his face and neck a scar the size of a silver half-dollar could be plainly seen on his neck. This scar was caused from cutting a bullet out of his neck, that he had received in a revolver duel in the Osage country with Lafe Shadly, who was killed in the Ingalls fight. I delivered my prisoner to the jailer at Guthrie. When I brought Dynamite Dick into the jail Bill Doolin's cell was in front of the main entrance, and as he saw the prisoner, he had a look of terror on his face and was very much excited. He asked me if he could speak to the prisoner. I motioned for Dynamite Dick to come up to the cell. The first words that Doolin said to Dynamite were, 'For God's sake, stand pat.' They talked for a few minutes in a whisper, and I could not catch the words. They then locked Dynamite Dick in a cell by himself.

The arrest of Dynamite Dick appeared to worry Doolin. He seemed to be very uneasy for some time. It was not long until Dynamite Dick overpowered the jailer, secured his keys, and released all the prisoners that wanted to go out. There were, as I remember it, thirteen prisoners escaped, including Bill Doolin. The field officers of Oklahoma were all directed to hunt down the escaped prisoners. Bill Tilghman and Heck Thomas requested Marshal Nagle to appoint the Dunn boys possemen for them to be used in hunting the outlaws. Mr. Nagle did not like to give the Dunn boys any official authority on account of their past record, but was finally persuaded to do so.

Bill Doolin's wife was staying with her father, a Mr. Ellsworth, about eighteen miles southeast of Pawnee near the Dunn settlement. Doolin had separated from the other prisoners after he escaped from jail at Guthrie. He had been hunted like a wild animal, and was dead on his feet. He finally got to his wife and was taken sick. She concealed him for about a week, expecting him to die at any time. The Dunn boys finally located him at the Ellsworth place, and reported to Heck Thomas, who immediately organized a posse of about ten men, including the Dunn boys. They surrounded the house in which Doolin was staying. Doolin must have had a presentiment that he was in danger, for he got up out of bed, had them saddle his horse, and staggered down a lane leading his horse, with his Winchester in his hand. Bill Dunn had squatted down in the edge of a patch of kaffir corn. Doolin walked right up to Dunn. As he did so, Bill Dunn fired both barrels of a number eight shotgun loaded with buckshot which struck Doolin square in the breast. This was the same shotgun that he used when he killed Charley Pierce.

Heck Thomas brought the dead body of Bill Doolin to Guthrie and had a picture taken of the naked body showing all the wounds in his breast. It was a ghastly picture.

I think all the other prisoners who escaped were finally recaptured. Dynamite Dick was shot and killed some time after by Bud Ledbetter in the Creek Indian country. Ledbetter was a Deputy United States Marshal under Martin Rutherford, who at that time was chief United States Marshal of the Muskogee District, and an excellent officer.

The Dunn brothers were now possemen for Heck Thomas and Bill Tilghman, and were riding over Pawnee, Payne, and Osage Counties heavily armed. Cattle were being stolen in all those counties. At one time forty cow hides were found near Bill Dunn's house on Council Creek with the brands cut out. Later on Sheriff Frank Lake and I arrested a stranger (I have forgotten the name he gave), who had just driven fifteen to eighteen head of cattle into Pawnee and sold them to old man Bolton, father of Chris Bolton. When we put the fellow in jail he told us that Bill Dunn and Amos Pierce, a noted thief, had stolen the cattle in Payne County and driven them up near Pawnee, then hired him to deliver them to old man Bolton. Then we got warrants for Amos Pierce and Bill Dunn.

I had received reliable information several times to the effect that Bill Dunn had sworn that he intended to kill me on sight, and some of my friends advised me to leave the country or he would sure get me. I kept a close watch when traveling over the country and always had one good man with me. An ambush was the only thing that I dreaded. In 1896 I was advised by a friend that Bill Dunn was in Pawnee. Judge A. G. C. Bierer was holding a session of district court at that time at Pawnee, and I was busy about town serving summons on jurors. I intended to keep my eyes open, of course, but I had so many, many things to do that day that I had almost forgotten that Bill Dunn was in town. I never expected him to attack me in the open, especially

while in town. But this is one time that I had my man
sized up wrong.

I had a forty-five-caliber Colt's revolver which I
carried on the right side with the clip over the waist
band of my trousers to hold the revolver up. I seldom
wore a cartridge belt when on duty in town. I had just
stepped out of a restaurant where I had been serving
subpœnas, and started to walk up the plank sidewalk
in the direction of the courthouse. Ten or twelve men
were standing about on the street, the weather was a
little chilly, and I had both hands in my trousers'
pockets. As I started up the street in a brisk walk, Bill
Dunn stepped in front of me. I had not seen him until
he spoke.

He says, 'Frank Canton, God d—— you, I've got it
in for you.'

He had his hand on his revolver, but had not drawn
it yet. When I glanced at his face I saw murder in his
eyes, and I knew that he intended to kill me. I drew
my revolver instantly and fired. The bullet struck him
almost square in the forehead. As he dropped he
pulled his revolver, which fell on the sidewalk near his
body. As he lay on his back dying, he was working the
trigger finger of his right hand. Then I walked over to
the sheriff's office and reported to Sheriff Lake. Some
of Bill Dunn's brothers were in town when Bill was
killed, but they immediately mounted their horses and
left the town.

Soon after this some of the citizens filed complaint
against the Dunn boys for cattle stealing and new

warrants were issued. Dal Dunn and John were still acting as United States officers under the direction of Heck Thomas. The people of Pawnee County demanded that they be arrested and brought to justice. They were scouting around over Osage, Pawnee, and Payne Counties heavily armed. Men, women, and children were afraid of them. I finally sent word to Heck Thomas that we held criminal warrants for the Dunn boys, and that I thought that it was his duty as an officer under the Department of Justice to bring these men in and deliver them to the sheriff of Pawnee County. Thomas ignored me absolutely, and did not even treat me with the courtesy to reply to my request. Up to this time I always had a great deal of respect for Heck Thomas, and considered him one of the best criminal officers in the Southwest, for I knew that he had been either directly or indirectly responsible for ridding the country of some very bad men. I never believed in killing a man in his sleep, nor shooting him in the back, no matter what his crime was, but I was always willing to believe that it was the murderous characters that Heck Thomas selected always as possemen who were more responsible for this dirty work than he was himself.

After I had notified him that the Dunn boys were wanted in Pawnee County, his actions proved to me that he intended to protect them under his authority as a United States Deputy Marshal in defiance of the Territorial laws, so I decided to make him show his hand.

PAWNEE COUNTY OFFICERS, 1897

We received information that Heck Thomas was in camp with eleven men on the Arkansas River about sixteen miles east of Pawnee. Sheriff Lake and I immediately picked a party of eight men, some of whom were the gamest men in the country, and all of whom were officers of experience. Among this number was Clarence Young, whom I always selected in a serious emergency. We had a good team and light wagon to haul our commissary supplies, excellent mounts, and plenty of ammunition. We left Pawnee after dark for the purpose of arresting the Dunn boys, for whom we had warrants.

We struck the Arkansas River at the Black Dog Crossing, where we found that Heck Thomas and his posse had broken camp, and pulled out through the Osage Hills in the direction of Skiatook in the Cherokee Nation. We followed their trail due east for about fifty miles, and went into camp in the hills. When we came down off the mountain the next morning, we were in sight of Lee Appleby's ranch in the valley of Hominy Creek. We found Lee Appleby at home. I knew that he was an intimate friend of Heck Thomas. He was also a good friend of mine. When I inquired if he had seen Heck Thomas and his men, he denied having seen them, but when I informed him that we had tracked the outfit up to his ranch, he admitted that they had been there for a few minutes but had left. We got dinner and fed our stock. While we were doing this Lee Appleby mounted his horse and rode off. He returned in about an hour. He told me confidentially, as a friend, that he had denied in the first place that Heck Thomas was there, for the reason that he did not want to see a clash between the two parties. He said that Thomas and his party had gone north in the direction of Pawhuska. We mounted our horses and circled the ranch. Soon we found their trail, and it was leading due south in the direction of Tulsa. We followed the trail about ten miles over the Delaware Flats, and then found that the tracks turned southwest in the direction of the mouth of the Cimarron River. We trailed the posse into the head of Shell Creek, where we lost it, and went into camp near the Arkansas River. The next morning we made a diligent search for the trail, but failed to find sign of any body of men. Occasionally one would find the tracks of a lone horseman coming out of the river bottom, and traveling east to the hills. We decided that we would cross back on the west side of the river. We found the river frozen over about halfway across on each side with a swift channel between the ice. We had great difficulty in crossing. The water was almost over the horses' backs. We got our saddle horses over all right, but the worst job was in getting the wagon and team out of the swift water up onto the ice. After tying our picket ropes to the wagon tongue and breaking the ice so that our mounts could get a foothold, we pulled the outfit over by the horn of the saddle without the loss of any stock. We could find no trace on the west side of the river of Heck Thomas and his party. What actually happened, as we learned later from a reliable source, was that the night we had our camp east of the Arkansas

River, Heck Thomas and his party were a mile below us in a bend of the river. By some means they found that we were close to them, and after looking at the river, decided that it was too dangerous to attempt to cross with their outfit, and rather than be caught in a trap in the bend of the river, they turned back east and scattered. Heck Thomas left them and rode to Vinita where he took the train for Guthrie. The Dunn boys left the country and have never been seen in Pawnee County since.

Bill Dalton was killed in the Chickasaw Nation by Dave Booker, of Ardmore and Los Hart; and Red Buck, the last one of the Dalton gang, was shot to death by officers and settlers in western Oklahoma. The most desperate and determined band of outlaws in the Territory had been wiped out completely and most of them had gone to appear before a higher court to answer for their crimes.

However, we still had many criminals in the country, cattle thieves, horse thieves, and whiskey peddlers, especially on the east side of the State where the whiskey peddlers made big profits on whiskey sold to the Indians in open defiance of the United States laws. This class of criminals were low, cunning, and contemptible. Generally, they were sneak thieves to begin with, which means that they were cowards. Occasionally some of them would put up a vicious fight when we ran onto them in the hills, provided they thought they had the best of it.

There was a noted whiskey peddler by the name of

Bill Buchanan, who operated along the border of the
Cherokee, Creek, and Osage Nations, and whom the
Department of Justice was anxious to have arrested.
At this time I had no authority to make an arrest in
the Creek Nation, as I had not as yet had my commission renewed, but I had jurisdiction in the Osage
country, and was watching for a chance to catch
Buchanan on the Osage side. Charley Colcord, who
at that time was a Deputy United States Marshal (but
is now a millionaire in Oklahoma City), suggested to
me that we make a trip to the Cherokee country and
break up this nest of whiskey peddlers of which Bill
Buchanan was leader. Mr. Colcord had an uncle and
several friends from Kentucky visiting him at this
time, whom he was anxious to take along on the trip to
give them an outing. We had a mess wagon and good
camp outfit, and each man had a mount except Mr.
Colcord's uncle who rode in a buggy. This was prior to
the discovery of oil in the Osage country and I believe
there was the finest black bass fishing that I have ever
seen in any country. We took the old Skiatook trail
running east through the Osage Nation. One evening
we went into camp rather early on a little creek in the
Osage hills called Boar Creek. While the rest of the
party were preparing camp and attending to the stock,
Wiley Haines and myself took our fishing tackle and
went up the creek a few hundred yards to see if the fish
would bite. It was not long until we had all the fish we
wanted. We brought in a string of sixteen black bass,
and I do not think that any of them would weigh less

C. F. COLCORD

than three pounds. They were very fat. We baked them in a large Dutch oven and had a royal dinner. Wild turkeys were plentiful and in fine condition. We could kill young turkeys (good frying size) with a shotgun. Our visitors certainly enjoyed themselves.

When we got over near the Cherokee line, we made a camp as a base to work from. We found a settler by the name of Smith near our camp who told us that the Creek Indians had gathered at the old Indian stamp grounds near the mouth of Bird Creek about ten miles south of Skiatook, and that their annual stamp dance would commence that night. We knew this was a good place to capture some of the whiskey peddlers for whom we had warrants. The Indian camp was located about eight miles southeast. After supper we selected five deputies, mounted our horses, took the settler Smith along to guide us to the camp, and rode out just at dusk. We left our Kentucky friends in camp, except one young man by the name of Courtland Lear, who said he had had some experience rounding up moonshiners in Kentucky, and would like to go along. As he had the appearance of a pretty game sport, we did not object.

We reached the Indian camp some time after dark, hitched our horses in the brush with a guard over them, leaving our Winchesters on the saddles, and concealing our revolvers under our coats. We found about four hundred Indians in camp. They were dancing the squaw dance as we came up, the squaws all dancing in a circle. Sam Childers, one of the most dangerous

Indians in the Creek Nation, was in charge of the camp. Several of his brothers and about one hundred of his kinsmen were with him. As we had our revolvers concealed, the Indians did not suspect that we were officers. However, we kept in the background for a time. We sent the guide Smith out through the camp to see if he could spot any whiskey peddlers. Soon he came back with the report that a whiskey peddler had a wagon and a barrel of whiskey in the brush at the edge of the Indian camp, and was selling whiskey to the Indians by the drink. We then moved over among the Indians where we could see all that was going on. A white man was in the wagon with a large barrel of whiskey. He was selling it to the Indians, men and women, as fast as he could draw it from a faucet with a tin cup, at twenty-five cents a drink. A white woman was seated in the hind end of the wagon with a Winchester across her lap, the hammer at full cock, watching every movement. I recognized the man at once. It was Bill Buchanan.

I knew that we were about two miles over into the Creek country where we had no authority to make an arrest. The only thing we could do was to watch the outfit all night, then capture him the next morning if he pulled back across the Osage line. We notified our men to watch the wagon and keep quiet. In a few hours pandemonium broke loose. The whole Indian camp was on the warpath, yelling, singing, fighting, and dancing war dances. I had seen Courtland Lear, the 'tenderfoot' from Kentucky, sitting on a log smok-

ing a cigarette, unconcernedly watching the Indians
fight all about him. Finally he stretched himself out on
the dry leaves and actually went to sleep. Smith, the
guide, had been patronizing the whiskey peddler himself. After he had got about a dozen under the belt, he
concluded that he could clean up on this bunch of
Indians. He singled out Sam Childers, the most powerful Indian in camp, and sailed into him. He knocked
Sam down twice, but when the Indian got on his feet,
he rushed onto Smith with a long, keen knife. The
white man ducked under the knife, but the Indian
then got a strangle-hold on Smith and threw him clear
over his head. When Smith fell to the ground, his feet
struck Courtland Lear in the face and woke him. Sam
Childers's brothers then made a murderous attack on
Smith. Courtland Lear had drawn his revolver to
shoot an Indian. We then closed in on the Indians and
had to beat them off with our revolvers to keep them
from killing Smith. He was the bloodiest man that I
ever saw, and was badly beaten up, but he was able
to ride back home. The Indians kept on drinking
whiskey and it was not long until they were all dead
drunk and helpless.

We then drew back to where our horses were in the
timber, and watched the wagon the rest of the night.
Just at daybreak the whiskey peddler pulled out
north with his team. We followed their trail leisurely
until they crossed the Osage line. Charley Colcord
and I then made a cut-off under cover of the timber
and dashed up onto the wagon before they knew we

were about. The woman was driving the team and Buchanan was lying down in the wagon bed. We had the dead drop on him and he surrendered without any show at resistance. We put handcuffs on Buchanan, took him and the woman to Guthrie, and they were both sentenced to the 'pen.'

Amos Pierce, whom I formerly mentioned as an accomplice of Bill Dunn in a cattle-stealing case, was convicted at Stillwater, and sentenced to the 'pen' for five years, after confessing his guilt and implicating his other two confederates. The stranger whom we arrested at Pawnee put up a cash bond of seven hundred and fifty dollars and left the country.

During this period of crime, from the time of the opening of Oklahoma to settlement up to 1897, the courts of the country were overrun with criminal work. It required a strong man to hold the position as Judge, or United States Commissioner, a man who had the backbone to defy the lawless element and to back up the field officers of his district, but in those days as a general rule our judges, commissioners, and prosecuting attorneys were on the dead square. Some of them were men of great moral courage.

There was a young man by the name of C. J. Wrightsman for whom I have always had the greatest admiration. He was, I think, the youngest member of the first legislature in Oklahoma, and was the first member who ever introduced a bill to prohibit gambling in Oklahoma. He carried his measure to a successful issue in the face of great opposition. This law was always called the Wrightsman bill. After the Cherokee Strip was opened, he was elected county attorney of Pawnee County, and later on was United States Commissioner in that district. During his administration outlawry was at the top notch. Mr. Wrightsman was absolutely fearless in the discharge of his duty. His life was threatened more than once, but he was never known to shirk his duty as an officer, but was always fair and impartial in his ruling. When the lawless element found that they could not bluff him, they had more respect for him than ever, which is always the case. Later on Mr. Wrightsman made a large fortune in the oil business in Oklahoma, and now lives in Tulsa.

The United States law prohibiting the sale of liquor to Indians and introducing liquor into an Indian reservation was enacted by Congress for the protection of the Indian, and also for the protection of white people, especially women and children, who live in an Indian country, from drunken Indians crazed by liquor. This was a good law if properly enforced by the United States Marshal. When a whiskey peddler was caught selling liquor to Indians in the Indian country, he was guilty of two charges, one for disposing of liquor, the other for introducing liquor into the Indian country. There was a certain class of Deputy United States Marshals in the country who took advantage of this law for their own benefit, and abused it most shamefully. For instance, many travelers passed through the Indian country driving a team and wagon,

camping out, and who would sometimes lay over for a
few days to fish and hunt, and would often carry a
bottle of good liquor with them for a morning's dram.
The class of deputy mentioned was always watching
for these travelers' camps, to hold them up, or stop
them on the road, and if they found as much as a half-
pint of liquor they would arrest the parties, take them
before a United States Commissioner, and get their
fees for bringing them in. The Deputy Marshal would
also confiscate the team, wagon, and all firearms of the
traveler, and after advertising the same for a certain
length of time, he would sell the outfit at public auc-
tion, and receive one half the proceeds for having informed on the party. This dirty work caused many
honest men an endless lot of trouble and expense. It
was never the intention of our General Government
that this law should be enforced in any such way. It
was thought that the officer making the complaint
should know if the defendant was a criminal, or not,
and should use good judgment in making the arrest.
The United States Commissioner could not discrimi-
nate under the law, therefore the best he could do was
to sentence the defendant to a minimum fine.

There was another law that was more outrageously
abused by these tin horn deputies than the liquor law,
that was called the timber law. The law under the
Interior Department prohibited the cutting of timber
on government land. When this law was enacted, the
General Government thought they were passing a law
which would help and protect the settlers in building

homes for themselves, and developing the frontier. The purpose of the law was to prevent contractors from cutting timber off government land for speculation. I presume they overlooked the fact that they had made no provision for the actual settler to cut timber on his own claim before he had proved up on it, and obtained title from the Government. Under the homestead law it would usually take the settler from three to five years to meet all the requirements of the Department and receive a patent from the Government on his home. When the settlers took claims, some of them had a great deal of timber on them. The settlers had to use this timber for fuel, building fences around their farms, and houses to live in. The law required that they should have a certain amount of improvement on their homestead before they could secure title. When they commenced to cut this timber to improve their own homes, the class of deputies referred to above, who did not have the nerve to arrest an outlaw, would make complaint against the settler for violating the timber law, get warrants, and swoop down on them and arrest and bring them in by the wagon load. They were usually fined ten dollars and released to walk home. But the deputy got the same fees that he would have received had he arrested a train robber. The settlers may have been technically guilty, but my sympathy always went to them, and I never arrested one of them on this charge in my life. The work of this class of officers in Oklahoma created such bitter feeling against the United States Marshals' force and even the Federal courts of the country, that the prejudice among the old settlers has not entirely died out. I have always regretted that the class of men that I have mentioned should have ever been permitted to carry a commission as a Deputy United States Marshal, for they were a detriment to the majority who were a brave and loyal body of officers. My honest opinion is that had it not been for the Deputy United States Marshals and the territorial officers of early days an honest man could not live in Oklahoma to-day.

By 1897 all of the principal bands of outlaws in Oklahoma had been broken up, the criminal work had reached the minimum, and had become monotonous to me. There was still a great deal of petty work for an officer to do, but it was a class of work that did not appeal to me, so I began to lay my plans to find a new field in which to operate.

CHAPTER VII

TO THE FAR NORTH

MR. P. B. WEARE, of Chicago, for whom I formerly worked in Nebraska City, was general manager of the North American Trading and Transportation Company in Alaska. They had trading posts on the Yukon River from Dawson to St. Michael. They had a string of river steamers on the Yukon, and also several ocean steamers that ran from St. Michael to Seattle. The Alaska Commercial Company was also in the same business. These two companies furnished all the food supplies used in the interior of Alaska. In 1896 the famous gold discovery on the Klondike had been made by George McCormick, a squaw man, who was fishing with a band of Siwash Indians, when he found coarse gold in the shallow bed of the Klondike River near where Dawson, N.W.T., now stands. This was the richest placer-gold discovery ever made in North America. Many thousands of people flocked into Alaska the same year, but the big stampede came in 1897.

The company for which Mr. Weare worked, and the O. and C. Company, had trading posts on the Yukon River from Dawson to St. Michael, and a string of river steamers on the Yukon, and also ocean steamers plying from St. Michael to Seattle and San Francisco, prior to the great gold discovery. On the Klondike there was virtually no law in the interior of Alaska except the law of right and wrong between man and man, which was most rigidly enforced by the few pioneers and miners who occupied the country at that time. These rugged frontiersmen who were three thousand miles from civilization made laws that were as binding in their settlements as an act of Congress would be in the States. Their principle was a 'square deal,' and as long as their law did not conflict with the statutes of the United States, our General Government did not interfere with them. Their system of adjusting disputes and for punishment of crime was about as follows:

When a crime was committed it was reported to the recorder of the mining camp. A complaint was then written out. If they had no paper they would use birch bark. The accused was then arrested by order of the recorder, and a miners' meeting was held. A jury of twelve men was summoned. The recorder would then appoint one prominent man to defend and one to prosecute the defendant, who would get a fairer trial than any man is allowed under our laws in the States. But if he were found guilty of a capital crime, such as murder for the purpose of robbery, or stealing grub from a cabin, his punishment was terrible, swift, and sure. The latch string on the cabin door was always on the outside to hungry travelers who were welcome to enter and cook a meal, but they were not supposed to carry anything away with them. If they did, they took their own lives in their hands. In those days the criminal had a horror of miners' meetings. The result was that provisions of all kinds, sacks of gold dust worth thousands of dollars, were perfectly safe in the cabin while the owner was out working in his mine.

But conditions changed after 1896. The big gold discovery on the Klondike had brought thousands of people to Alaska, and some of them were the worst criminals in the world. Gamblers, thugs, and cut-throats from the Pacific coast had gone in, not with the intention of mining, but for the purpose of robbing the honest men who had been lucky enough to strike it rich. The original miners in the country soon found that they were not strong enough to control the element by miners' meetings as they had always done in the past. Lawlessness had become so common along the Yukon River that the transportation associations called upon the President to send troops into the interior of Alaska to protect the interests of the country.

In the spring of 1897 Mr. P. B. Weare wrote me a letter from Chicago requesting to know if I would accept a position as Deputy United States Marshal in charge of the Yukon River District in Alaska. He stated that his company and the A. C. C. Company would each pay me a good salary while I remained in Alaska, and that he would have Mr. J. M. Sharp, of Idaho, who was then United States Marshal of Alaska, stationed at Sitka, appoint me Deputy United States Marshal for the Interior of Alaska so that I would be authorized to make arrests anywhere in the Territory. I had been anxious for some time to see Alaska, and I thought this a good chance. I knew the salary paid the Marshal of Alaska was very small, but the General Government paid all his expenses, which I later found was a big item. However, the salary offered me by Mr. W. was very satisfactory, and I concluded to accept the position and immediately notified Mr. W. to that effect, also United States Marshal Sharp at Sitka. Mr. Sharp notified me that I would be stationed at Circle City, Alaska, and that he would send my commission with instructions, blanks, and all records necessary for my office to Circle City. Then I began preparations to leave for the Northwest. I sent my wife and little daughter to Buffalo, Wyoming, to remain with my wife's parents while I was gone, and arranged with Mr. W. to send them a portion of my salary so that they might be well provided for during my absence. I found that Bill Painter, who was the first sheriff of Guthrie, Oklahoma, and Frank Kress, a former Deputy United States Marshal, were getting ready to go to Alaska. Frank Kress had been 'grubstaked' by some Oklahoma parties, and Painter was going in on his own responsibility. They were anxious to make the trip with me, and as I knew them both, I was glad to have them with me. We took the train at Perry, Oklahoma, in the latter part of July, 1897.

When we reached Seattle we found the town overrun with people outfitting for Alaska, every one headed

for the Klondike. Up to this time there had never been
any correct maps made of the interior of Alaska, and it
was very difficult to obtain any reliable information
about that country, but I found that there were two
routes to Dawson. One was to go from Seattle to
Skagway where they would unload the steamer, then
pack their outfit up over the Chilkoot Pass and down
to Lake Bennett which is the headwaters of the Yukon
River. They would build boats here, cross Lake Bennett, and shoot the White Rapids, then go down the
Yukon River to Dawson. This is the shortest route
from Seattle to Dawson. Most of the big crowd went
in over this trail. The other route was what was called
'going in over the water.' Leaving Seattle, out of the
Puget Sound, crossing the N. T. Ocean to Dutch Harbor on the Aleutian Islands, then across the Bering
Sea to St. Michael, then up the Yukon River one
thousand eight hundred miles to Dawson. This was
the longer route, and would take more time, but as I
had an annual pass on all ocean and river steamers
of the North American Trading and Transportation
Company, and managed to procure free transportation
for Painter and Kress, we decided to go in over the
water.

   We found several parties who had spent the winter
in Alaska. From them we got information as to what
we would need in the way of equipment in the frozen
North, including suitable clothing for an Arctic climate,
footwear of different kinds, woolen stockings and heavy
underwear, arctic socks lined with lambs' wool, and

several pairs of strong buckskin moccasins. We bought all kinds of tools that a pioneer would need in placer mining, building cabins, etc., in the wilderness where he could buy nothing. One old-timer who had been in Alaska gave me some good advice.

'Buy a Yukon stove and take it with you. You cannot build a fire on the ground in Alaska, for the reason that the whole country is a glacier, and the ice is so near the surface that if you build a fire on the ground you will soon have a hole of water by the melting of the ice which will put out your fire.'

I took his advice and bought a Yukon stove, which is a flat sheet-iron stove and very light. This is always carried on the dog sled when traveling in Alaska, and is an excellent stove for cooking a quick meal. I paid five dollars for it in Seattle, and refused one hundred dollars for it when I reached Alaska. We bought everything that we could think of that we thought we needed except food. We expected to buy that from the trading stores after we reached Alaska. However, when we got through we found that we were short of many necessary things that we should have brought in with us.

We left Seattle on the steamer Cleveland, which the North American Transfer and Transportation Company had chartered. Over two hundred passengers were aboard. The Cleveland was a very old steamer, and was considered an unlucky boat as she had been in a number of bad accidents along the coast of South America. However, she had been remodeled to some

extent, and looked so much safer than some of the
boats that people were taking passage on, that we decided to take our chances on her. We had pretty fair
weather until we reached the vicinity of Unimak Pass,
where we encountered a severe storm. This is a rugged
and dangerous coast, but our captain and crew kept
the old boat on top without serious accident. We
landed at the coaling station Dutch Harbor on the
Aleutian Islands to coal up, and remained there for
two days. We met quite a number of people at Dutch
Harbor who were returning from the Yukon River
country. They all reported that provisions were so
scarce in the interior that the supply the traders had
on hand would not be sufficient to feed the people
through the winter, and that there certainly would be
starvation on the Yukon before the next year's supply
could get in. After taking on a supply of coal we pulled
out across the Bering Sea, seven hundred and fifty
miles, to St. Michael on the mainland of Alaska. At
St. Michael we found many people from the interior
of Alaska who were waiting to get passage on an ocean
steamer to bring them back to the States. They all
reported that provisions on the upper Yukon were
getting scarce, and that flour was twenty-five dollars
per sack, and everything else in proportion.

The alarming reports of conditions up the Yukon
almost created a panic among the two hundred passengers who had landed at St. Michael. None of us
had provided food for the winter. The transportation
companies could carry only a limited amount of freight

for passengers, for every boat was loaded down with passengers whom they had contracted to take to Dawson. The agents of the two transportation companies told me that their companies had plenty of supplies for all of us at Circle City and Dawson, provided we could get up there before the Yukon River froze up. I was satisfied that the reports of starvation had been very much exaggerated. However, it was a serious proposition for the reason that it was now the 10th of September and the Yukon River usually began to freeze over by October 1. When this happened, and the ice began to run in the river, all steamers plying up the river had to get into winter quarters as quickly as possible. That meant that the steamer had to be run up into some side stream of the river proper and tied up for the winter. If the boat happened to be caught in the Yukon River, and the ice froze, they could winter there all right, but when the river broke up in the spring nothing could save the steamer from being crushed like an eggshell by the heavy anchor ice and icebergs that are forced down the swift current with tremendous power. There is one thing that a man must have to winter in Alaska, and that is good, strong food, and plenty of it. No man nor animal can stand starvation very long in that country with the thermometer down to sixty-five and seventy below zero.

We decided that the only safe proposition for us was to lay in a supply of provisions at St. Michael, and take the outfit up the Yukon. Sixty of us organized a stock company and bought a small steamboat. The name of

the little steamer was the St. Michael. We bought the
boat from a Catholic priest by the same name. We
paid him twelve hundred dollars cash for the steamboat. Then we bought forty-five tons of provisions
at St. Michael and loaded our boat. We hired two
experienced Eskimos who knew the channel of the
Yukon to act as pilots. A sufficient number of our
company volunteered to serve as a crew, engineer,
fireman, etc. It was eighty miles from St. Michael to
the mouth of the Yukon River. We started our little
steamer and cargo out about a week ahead, the rest of
us intending to come up on the next passenger boat
of the North American Transfer and Transportation
Company. Captain Patrick Henry Ray, and First
Lieutenant Dick Richardson of the United States
Army had left Seattle with me on the steamer Cleveland. They had orders to go to Circle City, Alaska, and
establish a supply station with the view of sending in
United States troops later to keep order in the interior.
They took in a large amount of provisions, army equip-
ment, etc. Captain Ray was not a stranger to the
Arctic regions. He had been ordered into Alaska
several years before this for the relief of shipwrecked
whalers in the Arctic Ocean. He was stationed at Point
Barrow for four years. I had known Lieutenant Richardson in Wyoming. He had been stationed at Fort
McKinney when I was sheriff at Buffalo, Wyoming.
The War Department had made special arrangements
with the North American Transfer and Transportation
Company to take these two officers with all their sup-

plies up the Yukon River. We left St. Michael on the steamer T. B. Weare, which was one of the most powerful steamers this company had. When we got out of the Bering Sea, and up into the Yukon River, we found the channel so swift that it required all the steam that our engine and boiler would stand to move the steamer up the swift current. At this time of year on the Yukon it begins to get dark very early in the evening. The captain of the steamer decided that it was not safe to attempt to travel at night, so we tied up, and traveled only in daylight. This caused us to lose a great deal of time, and I was very anxious to get to Circle City before the river froze up to enter upon the discharge of my duties as United States Marshal. We had a good captain and pilots who knew the river, but it was slow work fighting the swift current. We were very anxious about the St. Michael and our cargo of provisions, and expected to overtake them at any time. We could not believe that a tenderfoot crew could ever take this little boat up the river, especially after our steamer with her powerful machinery was having such a struggle to stem the current. We passed the mouth of the Koyukuk River, which is one of the large northern tributaries of the mighty Yukon. We found an Indian village here where we landed long enough to lay in a supply of dried salmon meat and buy some snowshoes, furs, etc., for winter use. The natives, some of whom could speak broken English, told us that the St. Michael had passed going up the river two days before. This was good news. After we had passed the

mouth of the Tanana River we commenced to meet
slush ice floating down the river. This meant that our
hopes for reaching Circle City or Dawson that fall had
gone glimmering. The next thing to do was to find
some side stream in which we could anchor our boat
and get into winter quarters as quickly as possible.
However, we had to catch the St. Michael to get our
provisions and outfit. We landed our boat on the bank
of the river one evening and took on a good supply of
spruce pine wood for making steam, then decided to
make a night's run up the river. We got along all right,
but had to move slowly. The next morning about daylight in rounding a bend in the river, we came in sight
of the St. Michael. The little steamer had on a full
head of steam and was bravely fighting the swift current and ice. They were glad to hear our whistle when
we signaled for them to stop. We found the men and
boat in good shape. They had made a remarkable
record for a small steamer and without an accident.
We were now about seven hundred miles up the Yukon
River and about eight hundred miles below Circle City.
Our Eskimo pilots told us that the mouth of Big
Minook Creek was fifty miles above and that it would
be a good place to winter. Another inducement for
putting in the winter on Minook Creek was the fact
that gold had been discovered on Little Minook Creek,
although the country had not been prospected very
much by white men. This part of the Yukon River was
called the 'Ramparts.' The bed of the river was a canyon running through the lofty mountains for about

seventy-five miles. The water in the river was from one
hundred to three hundred feet deep, and about a mile
wide. When we reached the mouth of Minook Creek
we found that a white man by the name of Al Mayo
had a store there. He was an independent trader. He
had been living on the Yukon for twenty-four years,
and had an Indian wife and several children. Also we
found that about fifty passengers who had come by way
of Skagway and Dawson had landed at Minook and
were building cabins expecting to prospect for gold
through the winter. We found a safe place to anchor
the St. Michael. Most of the passengers on the steam-
ship T. B. Weare decided to stop at Minook Creek.
Captain Ray and Lieutenant Richardson decided to go
on up to Fort Yukon one hundred and forty miles
above, where there were some good, comfortable log
cabins already built, in which they could store their
government supplies, provided they could make the
trip before the river closed. The ice was running
heavier all the time, but the captain of the steamer
Weare said he thought he had a fighting chance at
least to get through. After we had unloaded all our
equipment on the beach the T. B. Weare left us. They
reached Fort Yukon just before the ice closed the
Yukon for navigation. This place was called Fort
Yukon although there had never been any military
forces stationed there. I think it had formerly been
a station for the American Fur Company.

The next thing was to build cabins and get our supplies under cover as quickly as possible. There were

about two hundred passengers who had landed there
for the winter. Among this number were some twenty
white women. We got out our axes, saws, and other
tools, and all went to work to build a village in the
wilderness thousands of miles from civilization. Bill
Painter, Frank Kress, and myself decided to build one
cabin large enough for three of us. There was plenty of
spruce pine near by. This timber in that part of Alaska
did not grow large as a rule, on account of the glacier ice
being so close to the surface. The trees would average
about the size of an ordinary stove pipe, but they were
tall and straight, and made excellent poles for building
a cabin. We found the surface of the ground the same
as it is all over the most of Alaska, covered with a thick
growth of spongy moss called reindeer moss. This is
what the moose and wild reindeer (caribou) feed on in
winter, and is very nutritious. The surface of the
ground is very rough, with tufts of moss and grass
everywhere, called 'negro heads,' which leave holes
between. In the summer this moss and the holes are
full of water. We planned to build our cabin fourteen
by eighteen feet. First we scraped the ground off,
making a level place for a foundation. After we got the
muck and dirt cleaned off, we were on the solid ice.
Then we put down four poles for a foundation, cutting
a notch in the end of each pole for the next one to fit
into. We then put a thick layer of moss along on top of
the first poles, letting the next pole mash down into the
moss. We built the walls up in this way to the proper
height; then used smaller poles for a roof, which we

covered first with moss, then a thick layer of dirt and
muck. We soon discovered that we had no nails. This
was one thing that we had overlooked in Seattle when
we bought our outfit. As we could not get a nail in the
camp, I could not figure out for some time how we could
finish, and put in a door, window, and floor without
nails. But the old saying that 'necessity is the mother
of invention' is a true one, I think. I thought of a plan
that I believed would work, and proceeded to try it
out. We had a number of large pine boxes that our
goods were shipped in, and carefully took the pieces
apart to use in making a door, saving what few nails we
found in the boxes. When these were gone we used
a brace and bit to bore a hole, then drove in wooden
pins which appeared to hold as well as nails. We made
a good solid door. Then we picked out good, straight
poles for the floor. After pinning down both ends of
each pole we used a foot adz to hew the poles off flat
and smooth, which made a good, solid floor. We had
no window pane, of course, but we sawed out a small
window in the side of the cabin and covered it with
a white cloth that had once been a flour sack. This
helped considerably. But our worst disappointment
was yet to come. When we started in to put up the
sheet-iron stove that I bought in Seattle, I found that
we had no stove pipe for it. I had overlooked entirely
the matter of buying pipe for the stove. Something
had to be done. We could not get along without a
stove. I happened to think that the pipe used on these
sheet-iron stoves was about the same size as a tomato

can. We had brought in a good many cases of canned tomatoes. We opened a lot of cans and found that they would fit on the top of the stove. We melted off both ends of the cans, then slipped one can over the edge of the other until it was long enough to go up through the roof. Then with some fine wire that we had dug up that something had been packed with, we wrapped the cans closely so the smoke could not escape. We then made a fire in the stove and found that we had an excellent stove pipe which we used all winter. I appreciated this little sheet-iron stove more than anything that I took into Alaska with me. Many people in the camp had come in without stoves or dishes of any kind. We let these people cook on our stove while we were in camp, but when we were out on a trip with dog teams we had to take the stove with us. These people finally took two empty coal-oil cans, wired them together after melting out one end, and used them for stoves. They used the same kind of pipe that we did, and got along very well. They utilized every piece of tin they could get to make tin plates, spoons, and cooking utensils. We had built our cabin for comfort in the coldest climate. When it got cold enough to freeze, the wet moss in the walls of our cabin and on the roof froze up solid, which made the cabin almost airtight. We had to put a ventilator through the top of the roof to give us fresh air. When this job was completed we had the most comfortable quarters in the camp.

The next thing was to build a *cache* for our provisions, and get them out of our way. The *cache* is as necessary to a miner in Alaska as a cabin to live in. They are built by setting four posts in the ground about nine feet apart, forming a square, the posts to be about eight feet high. A platform or floor is then made on top of the posts, the walls are run up some five or six feet above the floor like building a cabin, and a good roof put on to keep the snow out, a door is put in, and you can get into this storeroom only by climbing a ladder. It is absolutely necessary to take all those precautions to keep the dogs from stealing the grub. The Eskimo dog has one fault, and one only. He is a notorious thief, and will steal anything on earth that he can eat. I have heard that they have been known to climb a ladder and enter a *cache* when the door was left open, and steal a ham or side of bacon. I have never seen one of them 'pull off' this stunt, but I do not doubt that it is true. However, they have so many good qualities that they can be forgiven for this one bad habit. There is no animal living that is so faithful and true to mankind as the Alaskan dog. In early days it was a capital offense to kill one of them maliciously.

After we had finished our *cache* we stored all of our provisions away for winter use. All canned goods, meats, and everything else freeze up solid in winter, but so long as they are kept frozen they are not damaged in the least. Even our coal oil would freeze partially. We had a good supply of salt pork and beans, which is an excellent proof of a cold country. We would slice up the salt pork, parboil it to make it fresh, and it would make excellent food. We used strong, black tea, but not much coffee. The tea is much better in a cold climate. I noticed that the black tea was used altogether by the natives.

When every one had finished the cabins and moved into winter quarters, we held a meeting and named the little village Rampart City. I had sent out a letter by Captain Ray reporting to the Attorney General at Washington, D.C., to the effect that the Yukon had closed to navigation and caught me at Minook Creek, and that I could not report for duty at Circle City until the next spring. I requested Captain Ray to send this letter on as soon as the ice in the river froze hard enough to hold up a dog team. Also I sent a letter to my wife and little daughter at Buffalo, Wyoming. I knew I would not have much official work to do in the Minook Creek district, so I planned to put in the winter prospecting for gold. There were several old miners on Little Minook Creek who were working placer mines that were paying them very well. Although there had not been any very large discoveries like the Klondike made, we had seen enough to give us the gold fever and every one in camp was anxious to get out on a stampede, and secure a claim.

CHAPTER VIII

A STAMPEDE FOR GOLD

THERE was an educated Indian by the name of Minook who had attended school at one of the Catholic missions on the Yukon River, and had lived in this vicinity all his life. Minook Creek was named after him. He was considered very reliable. He told us that the Indians found gold nuggets on the head of Big Minook Creek several years before, but that there had been no prospecting done up in that region. Al Mayo, the trader, corroborated this statement. One evening some parties who had been hunting moose came into camp and reported that they had discovered gold on the head of Big Minook Creek, and exhibited some of the coarse gold which they claimed they had found. This report was all that was needed to start a stampede. Every man in camp wanted to stake the first claim. Some of them started out on the hike with what grub they could carry in their pockets, and only half-clad for such a trip. It was about twenty-five miles to where the gold was supposed to have been discovered. The weather was getting cold, but we had not had any snow as yet. Therefore we could not travel with dog teams, but we had pack straps used for carrying a pack on the back. Seven of us started out together. Each man carried a pack weighing about seventy-five pounds, including rations for a week, two blankets, a small trail

axe, tobacco, matches, etc., and most of us wore heavy
gum boots, the tops reaching up to our hips. The men
in our party were Bill Painter, Frank Kress, Tucker,
two Chicago men, one other, and myself.

We started out on an old caravan trail that led
directly up Big Minook Creek. In the afternoon it
commenced a slow, drizzling rain. We had great
difficulty in traveling through the nigger heads and
swamps. The rain had soaked through our packs,
making them so heavy that we could hardly stand up
under them. We went into camp after dark completely
worn out. We found that there were places partially
dry, and after considerable time we found a spot under
a spruce pine tree that was not covered with water.
We made a small fire and fried some bacon and had
a cup of strong, hot tea. Our fire soon went out and we
spread out our wet blankets and turned in to get a little
rest at last. The next morning it was very cloudy and
still raining. We were all as wet as rats, but got a hot
breakfast and felt better. We supposed that it would
soon stop raining, and the sun would come out again
the same as in other countries. Had we known anything about the climate in Alaska at that time of the
year, or had known what we had yet to face, we would
not have risked our lives to go any farther for all the
gold in Alaska. We worked our way on up the creek,
over the tundra, nigger heads, thickets, and windfalls,
until all sign of any trail had disappeared. We used our
small axes to cut a trail through the alder brush and
network of dry pine poles that had decayed and fallen

in every direction which made it almost impossible to proceed. The creek was very crooked, and in order to keep our course we were compelled to cross the creek many times. The water was as cold as ice, but seldom came up higher than our hips. However, it was so swift that we could hardly stand up in it. We made our second camp for the night up on high ground where we found some dry spruce pine timber and plenty of birch bark. Soon we had a good fire going. This birch timber in Alaska grows almost everywhere. When the bark is stripped off, the tree will burn almost like coal oil. It has been a godsend to many gold-hunters in Alaska who had to build a fire quickly or freeze to death. We had to move our fire several times on account of the thawing of the ice under the surface, but finally got our clothing pretty well dried out. The Indian, Minook, had told us that gold nuggets had been found at the mouth of a deep canyon on Minook Creek in the lofty mountains, and that when we got up the creek high enough to see red fish, we were in a few miles of the place where the discovery was made. While the boys were getting supper I walked down to the creek and in a large hole of water that was clear as crystal, I saw for the first time the golden trout of Alaska, which is the most beautiful fish that I have ever seen. They are about the size of the brook trout in Colorado and Wyoming. The spots on them are scarlet, the tail and fins are also a beautiful bright red. They are a very game fish and when cooked have a most excellent flavor. It was a great disappointment to me that I had no fishing tackle, but none of us had thought of bringing a fish hook.

After supper we cut spruce pine boughs to sleep on. I do not think I ever was so tired in my life. The wet packs that I carried had got so heavy that I could hardly stagger under them, and the weight of my heavy gum boots made me feel as though my hips were disjointed. The next morning we were all stiff and sore. The rain had stopped, but the clouds were very dark and heavy, and the air much colder. We calculated that we could not be over five miles from the place where we wanted to stake claims, so we decided to lighten up our packs by leaving our blankets and a part of our provisions. We took along some sea biscuits, black tea, and some extract of beef for making beef tea, and pulled out on the trail. We still had to cross the creek every few hundred yards, but as the water had not yet begun to rise, we could still wade it. After we had traveled about three or four miles, snow commenced falling in heavy flakes. We had just passed the mouth of a small creek, a tributary of Big Minook. Tucker and one other member of the party had dropped behind the rest of us for some reason, and when they came to the mouth of this creek they followed it up into a large canyon, thinking they were on the main creek behind us. It was some time before we missed them, and we still thought they would follow us up. We pushed on up Minook Creek which was getting more narrow all the time until we finally reached a tremendous, deep, narrow gorge with mountains on each side, the tops of which were up above the clouds. We selected a place under some large spruce pine trees to camp and wait for Tucker and his partner to catch up with us. The heavy snow continued to fall. It was not yet cold enough to freeze, and the wet snow was melting as it fell, which made traveling nearly impossible. We managed to start a fire in some big logs that we dragged up under the trees, although the water was pouring down from the spruce pine boughs overhead like a shower bath. We got supper, and by gathering armfuls of birch bark and dead pine poles we kept the fire alive all night. About midnight the water commenced to roar in the canyon of Minook Creek. We knew what this meant. The rain and heavy snow in the lofty mountains, which could not go into the ground on account of the ice near the surface, were pouring down into the canyon of Big Minook Creek in torrents. We were facing a most desperate situation. There was only one way for us to get back to camp, and that was to go back over the same trail that we had traveled, and this meant that we would have to cross the creek many times as we had done before. We stood around the slim fire for several hours and talked over the situation, but no one could offer a solution as to how we could escape from the death trap that we were caught in. It was absolutely impossible to climb the steep mountains, and we had only enough grub to last two days.

Frank Kress and Painter had stretched themselves out on the ground to try to get a little sleep. The two Chicago men, who had never roughed it in their lives,

sat on a log near the fire, and as the roar of the swift
water in the canyon rose louder and louder their faces
blanched with terror. I have had many close calls in
my life, but I felt that this was the most serious proposition that I had ever been up against. I lay down on
the wet ground, pulled my oilcloth blanket over me,
and was soon asleep. At daylight the snow was about
three feet deep. We all looked at the creek, and found
that the gorge was a raging torrent, and as swift as
a mill race. The water was probably thirty to forty
feet deep, and still rising. We made some hot tea and
got breakfast. We had given up all idea about staking
any claims. From now on it would be a fight for our
lives. As Tucker and his partner had not shown up we
had about given them up for lost. Frank Kress was the
best woodsman in the party. He had worked in the
logging camps in Minnesota and Michigan. He remarked that he had thought of a plan during the night
that he believed might work. He said that he did not
dare to tell what it was until we tried it out. We
packed up at once. Kress led the way to the gorge, and
we all followed him. There were plenty of very tall
spruce pine trees or poles, about twelve inches thick at
the bottom, that grew close to the bank of the creek.
Kress picked out a tree opposite a narrow place in the
gorge, took his trail axe out and began chopping on it.
I could see then that his plan was to make a foot log to
cross on. He cut the tree in such a way that it fell
square across the creek, and lapped on the opposite
bank with room enough to hold. We all crossed over

safely by crawling on top of the pole like a coon. We then worked on down the creek until the mountains closed in, and we had to cross back by the same means. It was slow work cutting down trees with our little, short-handled trail axes, and each man took his turn at chopping and worked with a will. Sometimes we would miss our calculations by cutting a pole that would miss the opposite bank by probably a foot. It would then go down the swift current like a shot. At other times the pole would sag down in the middle and the water would run over it. But we took our chances, hung on to the limbs, and crawled over one at a time. It was a hazardous game. We knew that it meant certain death to the man who slipped off the pole into the icy current, but it was the only chance. At times the weight of a man would sink the middle of the pole under the water two or three feet. Then it was a fight to keep from being washed off.

We made about two miles the first day, and went into camp almost exhausted. Our clothing was completely soaked with water, but fortunately we had kept our matches dry by having carried them in a small waterproof box. The snow had stopped falling, and it was growing cold very fast. We found some large flat rocks upon which we made a good, hot fire, and soon got warmed up. We had managed to hang onto what little grub we had left. We cooked supper and ate sparingly in order to make our grub hold out until we got down to our *cache* where we had left our blankets and outfit on the trip up the creek. We had almost given up all hope of ever seeing Tucker and Powers, his partner, for they were both young men who had been born and bred in the city and had never had any experience in roughing it. We kept the fire burning all night, but as we had no blankets it was too cold to sleep much. The temperature next morning was about freezing. The snow had stopped melting and was about three feet deep. After breakfast we pulled out and after a short hike were compelled to cross back over the gorge again. After cutting several trees we found one that reached across. We made a landing but all got soaking wet. We now found that we were getting down below the canyon, and the creek was too wide to cross on a foot log. But the bottoms were also getting wider and as we were now on the same side of the creek that our *cache* was on, and also our camp, we hoped that we could work our way down without having to cross the creek again. The snow was so deep that without snowshoes it was almost impossible to travel and required all the strength and energy that one possessed to keep moving. I noticed that Captain Bill Painter was lagging behind. I had the party wait several times until he came up. He would always say that he was all right and would never admit that he was played out. Captain Painter was about seventy years old and had been a remarkably vigorous man. I think he was the gamest man that I ever met, but the terrible hardships and exposure that we had passed through for several days were too much for him, although he was too game to admit it. Finally he dropped behind. I called him

several times but received no answer. I told the boys
to stop and make a fire, boil some tea, and that I would
go back to see what had become of Painter. I followed
the trail back about one half mile and found him
stretched out on the snow sound asleep. When I woke
him up he said he was all right, and begged me to leave
him. I talked to him for some time, but could not per-
suade him to move. I saw that he was almost exhausted but I thought if I could make him angry I
might arouse his ambition so that he would make an effort to get into camp. I insulted him, cursed him, and
abused him until he got up on his feet. Then he tried to
brain me with his trail axe. I expected this and dodged
the blow that he aimed at my head. He said that he
was a better man than I was, and could walk me to
death, and that if I did not believe it to follow him.
This was what I had wanted him to do and I followed
him. When we had walked about halfway to camp he
sank down in the snow. I could see that he was 'all in.'
He said that he could go no farther and begged me to
leave him, that he did not care to live any longer. He
asked me to forgive him for striking at me with his axe,
and to take a message to his family in Oklahoma. I
told him that I had no idea of leaving him and that I
intended to get him in. He was a larger man than I am,
but I got him on my shoulders and carried him into
camp. After he had drunk a tin cup full of strong, hot
tea, and eaten some bacon, he acted like a different
man.

While we were eating dinner we heard some one

shout for help back over our trail. We all sprang to our feet and saw a man staggering along the trail about thirty yards away. We called to him and when he approached us we saw that it was Powers who had got separated from our party three days before. His face and hands were so badly swollen from cold that we could hardly recognize him, and his clothes were almost torn off of him. He appeared to be almost insane, and we could not understand anything he said until we got him warmed up and gave him something to eat. He was almost famished and ate nearly everything in camp. After this he talked more rationally.

His story was that when he and Tucker got separated from us they followed up a canyon, thinking they were on Big Minook Creek. When they found out their mistake they could not find their way out of the canyon on account of the blinding snow. He said that Tucker fell in the creek in the darkness, and came near drowning, and that they had got all their matches wet. They lost one of their packs with all their grub except a few sea biscuits they carried in their pockets. They made a wet camp the first night without any fire. He said that they remained there all the next day and the next night without any fire and with hardly anything to eat, and that Tucker was so weak that he could not stand on his feet. When Powers realized that he could do nothing any longer for his partner, he left him and started down the creek to try to find help. He said that he was compelled to swim the creek twice to keep from having to climb the mountains, and by a miracle he struck our trail and followed us to the camp. He calculated that it was about three miles to where he had left Tucker. I had taken a mind photograph of the landmarks as we went along the creek, and I was sure that our *cache* was only a short distance below where we were now camped. Young Tucker was my intimate friend, and, while I had no hope of finding him alive, I felt that it was my duty to go to him. I thought that if I could hold out to make the trip I could at least place his body so that it would be protected from the wolves and wolverines. I told our party what my intentions were and called for one volunteer to go with me. Frank Kress said that he would go. After making a close search all that we could find in the outfit in the way of grub was one little mug of extract of beef for making beef tea. I put this in my pocket and told the rest of the party to go on down the creek until they found our *cache*, where there were provisions and blankets; to wait there at least three days; then if we did not show up, they could go on to camp and report. Kress and I threw our light oilcloth blankets over our shoulders, took our trail axes, and pulled out on the back trail that Powers had made. His trail was very plain in the deep snow, but we had a dangerous task when we came to the place where he had swum the creek in a canyon. To avoid having to swim in the ice-cold water we worked our way around the canyon over the side of a precipice that overhung the canyon about one hundred feet above the water, and came down over the bluff and found his trail again where he took the

water. At this time of year in Alaska, or until the surface of the country freezes up solid, it is a most dangerous undertaking to attempt to climb the steep mountains. If you step on a rock on the side of a steep hill
which appears to be solid, it will give way with you.
A bush as large as the arm of a man will pull up by the
roots, if you swing your weight on it. The reason is
that the glacier ice is so near the surface that the trees
and brush cannot get much root. The sun is hot enough
in the short summer to melt the soil and muck above
the ice and everything is loosened up. This is the cause
of the dreaded avalanches in the lofty mountains.

We followed the trail of Powers which led us in a zig-
zag course to the dead body of Tucker, lying on his side
in the snow, his glassy eyes and haggard face turned
towards the trail taken by Powers. He appeared to
have been dead about four or five hours. We closed his
eyes, and covered the body with an oilcloth blanket.

It was now late in the evening and we were awfully
hungry and tired. We built up a good fire in the rocks,
made some strong, hot beef tea, and then laid in a supply of wood and prepared to spend the night. We took
turns sitting up through the night. One man kept the
fire going while the other slept.

It was a long, lonesome night, and the sad fate of
young Tucker had made such an impression upon my
mind that I could not sleep. He had been my room-
mate on the steamer Cleveland on our trip from Seattle
to St. Michael. He was a noble young man about
twenty-two years of age, and the only son of an old

gentleman who was a banker in Troy, New York. He
was very devoted to his mother and on the voyage over
wrote her many letters relative to the newspaper reports that many prospectors had perished on the trail,
and that there was a shortage of provisions. In order
to remove her fears, invariably he would tell her that
these reports were greatly exaggerated, and always
ended his letters with a promise to take good care of
himself. He was the first man in our party to perish.

The next morning at daybreak we selected a spot
near some tall pine trees to leave the body. We
scraped the ground off down to the solid ice, placed the
body on it, and wrapped our oilcloth blankets about it
securely, covering up the face entirely. Then we cut
some good-sized logs and made a pen around the body
some four or five feet high, put a top on it, and then
piled heavy rocks on it to hold it down so that no wild
animal could get it. We then cut notches in the trees
so that we could find the spot in the event that we
wanted to move the body in the future. We left about
noon for the return trip. It was now growing cold and
freezing all the time. We had the same tiresome trip
on our return, but by making a cut-off we managed to
shorten the distance considerably. We stopped occasionally to make some hot beef tea. This diet may be
all right for a convalescent in a hospital, but it has not
the staying qualities sufficient to keep a man alive very
long when he is on a hike in the rugged climate of
Alaska.

We passed the camp where we had left our party,

then took up their trail which we followed about a mile, and staggered into camp where the party was all waiting for us. The men got busy and cooked us a good, hot meal, bacon, canned beans, canned beef, sea biscuit warmed up in hot bacon grease, and strong, black tea. I do not think I ever enjoyed a meal so much in my life, for I was as hungry as a wolf. The boys had our blankets pretty well dried out and plenty of spruce boughs for bedding. I turned in soon after supper and did not wake for ten hours. After breakfast we packed up for the return trip to camp on the same trail that we had made going up. The deep snow made hard traveling through windfalls and nigger heads, but fortunately we had blazed the trees and did not have much trouble in keeping on the trail. About noon we met a relief party with dog teams and sledges, who had been sent out from our camp to hunt for us. Our friends were delighted to see us alive, and on our feet, but no better pleased to see us than we were to see them. They were shocked to hear of the death of young Tucker, who was a favorite with every one. They reported that two other men who had started out on the stampede had perished, but none of the party had gone up as high as we had.

We unpacked the sledges, unharnessed the dogs, and went into camp. They had brought a sheet-iron stove for cooking, plenty of good food, a quart of Scotch whiskey, a box of cigars, warm blankets, and several extra pairs of snowshoes. As we had almost everything we needed we decided to remain in camp and take a rest until the next day. While dinner was being prepared, we all made a good strong, hot toddy, and there was no question but that it hit the right spot. After eating what we all voted to be an excellent dinner we rested until noon the next day, then made an easy drive into camp.

I was glad to get back to our comfortable cabin. It took a week's rest to get the soreness out of my limbs. It was the hardest trip that I ever made in my life. To think of it now that it is all over, it seems to be a hideous nightmare. I thought I knew how to travel in the mountains, or anywhere else, and take care of myself, but this trip taught me a lesson that I shall never forget, and one that was worth a great deal to me during my stay in Alaska. I have traveled a great deal since, through the wilds of Alaska, by dog teams, and rivers, over the ice in the winter, and in all kinds of boats over the water in the summer, but I never suffered with cold and hunger as I did on my first trip in the stampede up Minook Creek. I had learned what to wear and how to take care of myself.

In the first place, it is almost impossible to travel across the country in the interior of Alaska in the summer, or in the fall before it freezes up, and the old-timers will not attempt to do it unless it be for a short trip. The mosquitoes will almost run a man crazy, for this is the original home of this pest. They do not go into winter quarters until the first snow comes in the fall. Then they go down into the moss under the snow and live in a torpid condition all winter. When the sun

begins to warm up the earth the next spring, the mosquito wakes up and is out hunting for you before all the
snow leaves. The country is alive with them then until
the snow falls again. The only protection from them is
a smudge or a fine wire net to pull down over the head
and face. The ordinary mosquito bar is useless. It is
also necessary to wear buckskin or leather gloves. The
way to travel in the summer is in a poling boat up and
down the swift streams that are tributary to the Yukon.
These little boats are made by the natives of walrus
skin and birch bark. The prospectors and miners make
them out of pine timber sawed out with a whip saw.

The proper footwear for summer is the mukluk, which
is made by the coast Eskimos from the hair seal that is
caught in the Bering Sea. The hair is all scraped off,
leaving the hide stiff like rawhide. The top reaching to
the knee, this makes a very light and serviceable boot
that can be worn all summer and is absolutely waterproof, and one pair will last all summer. There is no
place for gum boots in Alaska. They are a nuisance.
The footwear for winter is a good, strong pair of moccasins made of caribou skin. Leather shoes or boots
cannot be worn while traveling in winter in extremely
cold weather. Two pairs of socks are used, one pair of
ordinary woolen socks next to the feet, then a pair of
arctic socks lined with lamb's wool which reach up to
the knee are pulled on. The moccasin is made of soft
caribou skin which reaches up over the ankle and
usually has thick moose skin for the sole. This makes
a light, comfortable footwear which will not slip on the

ice. Gloves are never used in winter. Mittens made of moose skin with the hair on the inside are warm. They are clumsy, and resemble a pair of boxing gloves. In order to keep from losing them, a cord is worn around the neck with a mitten attached to each end which hangs down just below the hips.

After the Yukon River is frozen over and the ice is strong enough to bear up the weight of a man and dog team, there is a great deal of travel over the ice all winter, and after the trail is once broken the more travel there is, the better the trail gets. But there is one great danger that the traveler must face and always guard against when traveling over the ice on the Yukon River in winter, and that is the air holes in the ice. The water will sometimes come up through the air holes and spread out over the ice under the snow, and if the traveler is not careful he will drive his dog team into the water and get their feet wet, and also get his moccasins wet. When this happens he must get out of the water as quickly as possible. Then if he has an extra pair of moccasins and dry socks tied on top of his pack on the sledge as he should have, he can put them on before his feet freeze, but he will have to work pretty fast. When a dog gets his feet wet in winter the water will freeze between his toes in a few minutes. The Eskimo dog will sit down and lick the ice from between his toes with his tongue, and the driver cannot make him get up until he has entirely cleaned his feet of ice.

In winter, when dogs are badly needed, a good Huskie or Malemute dog is worth two hundred dollars.

It takes six dogs to make a good team. They can pull twelve hundred pounds over the ice. Their native food is fish, but they will eat almost anything that is eatable. When traveling with a dog team, we always carried a sheet-iron stove and a small tent, and nearly always had to go into camp long after dark on account of the short daylight in winter. When we stopped to camp, the first thing was to pitch the tent on top of the dry snow, then cook supper for the hungry dogs first. Usually we fed them rice and pork boiled together, and sometimes we cooked dried salmon when we had a good supply of it. We always fed them all they wanted at night and gave them only one meal a day when traveling. After eating they will curl up on the dry snow and rest until morning when they are ready for the harness again. It is almost impossible to get one of them to come into a tent unless he goes in to steal something to eat when no one is about.

These dogs will never leave a man on the trail if they are treated kindly and can get enough to eat. They do not bark like the ordinary dog, but howl like the wolf. They become attached to a man who will treat them with kindness, but I have known them to turn on a brutal driver when he was cruelly beating them, and tear him to pieces.

The long winter nights in Alaska are very monotonous until one becomes accustomed to the climate. It begins to get dark at three o'clock in the afternoon, and daylight comes at ten o'clock in the morning. Therefore, one must travel and work a great deal without daylight. It never gets pitch dark north of the Arctic Circle, and is more like twilight. The atmosphere is so pure that with snow on the ground one can distinguish an object for some distance, and we would often have the aurora borealis, or northern lights, at night, which would illuminate the heavens like a powerful electric searchlight. Words cannot express the magnificent beauty of the northern lights seen north of the Arctic Circle. They first appear in the north at the top of the horizon, then gradually rise and spread out in beautiful waves until the entire space under the stars is crowned with this brilliant light, which is every color of the rainbow. During this display the spruce pine trees, birch, and alder bushes that grow in the lofty mountains appear to be covered with millions of flashing and scintillating diamonds of every color that can be seen in the northern lights. This is caused by the reflection of these brilliant lights on the frost and snow which covers the trees and underbrush. It is a beautiful sight which no one can ever forget.

There was a great deal of prospecting for placer gold in the Minook Creek district during the winter of 1897 and 1898, and several big stampedes were pulled off out of Rampart City, but no one found gold in paying quantities except certain miners who had claims on Little Minook Creek. Some of those men struck pay dirt and took out plenty of coarse gold. This fact proved that there was gold in that district, which flambeau kept the camp alive all winter.

Rex Beach, the author who made himself famous

writing Alaska stories, wintered with me at Rampart in 1897. At that time I do not suppose that he had any idea of ever writing a book. He was a handsome young fellow about twenty-four or twenty-five years of age, but he was a husky chap with plenty of backbone and nerve. I think he could stand up under a pack on the trail as long as any man that I ever met, and he was as good as the best on snowshoes.

It had been rumored for some time that Indian hunters had discovered gold and had brought in nuggets found on the head of tributaries to the Tanana River over the mountains about one hundred miles south of Rampart City. Beach, Bill Painter, and I decided to make a trip over there and stake claims. We had a good dog team for this trip, plenty of grub, our sheet-iron stove and small tent. We took the Indian trail up Hunter Gulch, over the divide, and down the Troublesome River where we found some fair prospects in a canyon where we all staked claims and named the creek 'Quartz Creek.'

After staking several more claims on different creeks, we laid in a supply of fresh moose meat, and started back home. One day we had been traveling from early morning until afternoon up a very steep grade trying to reach the top of a bold mountain. When we reached the top, which was above timber line, we found the old trail ran down a long slope which was an open slope about fifty yards wide. At the foot of this slope, about a mile from the top, was a mountain of snow that had drifted across the trail and appeared to be about one hundred feet high. On the right of this slope was a deep canyon which was probably a thousand feet from the rim of the precipice to the bottom of the canyon. After taking a look at the long, open slope in front of us, Beach bantered me to take a toboggan slide on the sled down the slope to the big snow drift at the bottom, as the open slope appeared to be free of any obstruction. I accepted this challenge to ride down on the sled.

We unhitched the dog team and turned them over to Bill Painter to lead down the mountain. Beach took his seat on the sled in front astride of the pack. I took my seat just behind him in the same position so that we could hold our feet up some eight inches above the snow. Then we headed the sled for the middle of the slope and turned it loose. After we got under headway we soon found that the grade was much steeper than we had any idea of. The slope was getting steeper, and the sled was gaining momentum so fast each second that I could scarcely get my breath. I am sure that the swiftest express train that I ever traveled on was slow compared with the gait that we were going. The fine snow almost blinded us, but as Beach was in front I was better protected from the flying snow, and in glancing over his shoulder I noticed that our sled had changed its course, and was heading straight for the precipice over the canyon on the right. I yelled for Beach to fall off, and at the same time I rolled off on the left side. I struck the soft snow on my shoulders. After turning about a dozen somersaults so fast that I

could not count them, I finally got on my feet just in
time to see a flying object strike the snowdrift four
hundred yards below. Beach had stuck to the sled.
When I rolled off on the left side, I think my weight
must have changed the course of the sled enough to
prevent it from shooting over the precipice into space
and landing in the canyon a thousand feet below.

When Beach saw his danger he had also turned the
sled by the motion of his body. However, when we
examined the track of the sled runners we found that
he had coasted along for some distance not more than
three feet from the edge of the precipice. He had then
steered the sled back into the trail on the slope and
struck the soft snowdrift below with such terrific force
that the sled made a tunnel into the snow about thirty
feet. I got to him as quickly as I could travel and supposed that he was almost smothered to death, as he and
the sled were entirely out of sight, but he had crawled
out in the open before I reached him, apparently all
right after his wild ride and miraculous escape from
death. We rested until Painter brought up the dogs.
In an hour we had dug the sled out of the snow and had
the dogs in the harness. We then took the trail down
the mountain to the head of Hunter Creek and went
into camp for the night. The next day we made an
easy drive to Rampart City.

It was now midwinter and we found it hard to kill
time during the long winter nights. The weather was
so cold that we could not do much hunting moose and
caribou. The barrel of a rifle would get so cold from

the frost that if you touched it with your bare hands
your fingers would stick to the gun-barrel. We sometimes had a chance to buy fresh moose meat from Indian hunters by paying fifty cents a pound. Occasionally we would have a dance to break the monotony.
There were some six or seven young married women in
the camp, and quite a number of half-breed Indian
girls in the Indian camp near by, who had been taught
to speak English in the mission schools down the Yukon
River. But the hardest thing to bear was the fact that
we could not hear from the outside. When the Yukon
freezes up, the interior of Alaska is more isolated than
South Africa, or was at the time that I was in there.
It was nine months before I received a letter from my
family, and we could not get newspapers at all. We
could send a letter out occasionally by giving it to some
mail carrier, and paying him one dollar a letter. He
would travel with a dog team up the Yukon and deliver
the mail at Dawson a thousand miles up the river. The
Northwest Mounted Police would then take the mail
across the country to Juneau or Skagway.

Windy Jim was considered the most reliable mail
carrier on the river. We had sent him up the river with
a thousand letters in the latter part of October, 1897,
paying him a thousand dollars. On account of severe
storms on the upper Yukon he did not return until
May, 1898. He brought back twenty-five hundred
letters from the outside for which we paid him twenty-
five hundred dollars more. No one refused to pay for
his letters, for we all knew that Jim had earned every

HAND-SLEDS AT THE HEADWATERS OF THE YUKON

cent of the money. However, many of these letters had been written about the time we left the States. We were very anxious to get late news for the reason that, from rumors picked up, we had heard that the United States was getting ready to declare war against Spain.

It was now about the middle of March. The sun had begun to have some effect upon the snow which caused it to settle so that traveling with sleds and dog teams was excellent. I had decided that the proper time had come for me to take a party and go back to the head of Big Minook Creek where I had left the body of young Tucker the fall before, and bring the body down to our settlement where we could give it a Christian burial. I soon organized a small party with good dog teams, and sufficient supplies. I led them back over the trail that we had traveled on our first stampede, but found traveling more difficult than we expected on account of the heavy snow drifts. The appearance of the country had changed so completely that nothing looked natural. Finally we worked up into a canyon which I was sure was the one in which Tucker had perished, for I recognized the familiar landmarks and mountains. We hunted an entire day for the spot where I had left him, and just as we had about given up all hope of ever finding the body I found one of the notches that I had cut with my trail axe in a spruce pine tree. From this mark I soon got my bearings. We found the body under about twenty feet of snow, frozen as hard as a rock. The little oilcloth blanket still covered his face and the corpse looked as natural as life. We wrapped a tarpaulin around the body and tied it securely to the sled. We had less difficulty on the return trip, as we had a good trail broken to follow. The temperature was about twenty-five degrees below zero, and we knew there was no danger of the fresh air affecting the appearance of the body.

We dug his grave eight feet deep on a hill overlooking Rampart City. The entire camp turned out at his funeral, and we found a minister in the party who conducted the services. I wrote the relatives of young Tucker in Troy, New York, and advised them of what disposition we had made of the body.

CHAPTER IX

THE RESCUE OF THE WALRUS

ONE day about the first of April 1898 Bill Painter and I were sitting in our cabin when a stranger pushed open the door and came in. After taking off his pack, he inquired for United States Marshal Frank M. Canton. When I told him that I was the man whom he was looking for, and invited him to take a seat, he said that he was captain of a steamboat called the Walrus, that he had gone into winter quarters the fall before about seventy miles below on the Yukon near the mouth of the Koyukuk, and had been there all winter in the ice. That he had a cargo of supplies to deliver at Dawson, and also had about a hundred and fifty passengers. There were some dead tough men in the party who dominated the entire camp, and they had taken possession of his boats and were now living off his supplies, and had planned a conspiracy to seize another small steamer that he owned called the Cora, load it with supplies, and as soon as the river broke up and the ice cleared they intended to take the Cora, load her with a good outfit, and go up the Koyukuk River and prospect for gold.

He said that he had heard of me as a United States officer, and had come to ask me to return with him and restore order in camp, and to take charge of the expedition until they reached Dawson.

I realized this was a big job for one man to tackle. While I had, of course, Uncle Sam to back me in the discharge of my official duty, yet I was the only United States officer on the Yukon for eighteen hundred miles, except one United States Commissioner who lived at Circle City. I had heard of this outfit down the river, and knew that there were some hard men in the party who were badly wanted in the States. But life at Rampart City had become so monotonous to me that I felt that nothing could be any worse. As there appeared to be a good chance for some excitement, I accepted the captain's proposition and told him that I would go down and remain with him until the ice went out of the river, then take charge of the outfit up the river as far as Circle City three hundred miles below Dawson, where I would then have to take charge of the United States Marshal's office.

I left Bill Painter in charge of our cabin, took my magazine Winchester with plenty of ammunition, and packed what other things I needed, and the captain and I left Rampart before daylight the next morning. We carried heavy packs, but the snow had begun to settle, and the trail was good. We made good time until the afternoon of the next day when the captain slipped on the ice and got a bad fall which sprained one of his ankles. It was a painful accident, but not serious, and as we were in about eight miles of the boats, I told the captain that I would push on ahead and he could come on at his leisure.

I came in sight of the camp before dark. The cabins

occupied by the hundred and fifty passengers had all
been built on an island in the tall spruce pine timber.
They thought this island was above high water mark,
but none of them had ever seen the Yukon break up.
The Walrus and the little Cora were not anchored in
the ice near the island, but up in the mouth of a side
stream where they would be protected from the crush
of ice when the river broke up. I did not go to any of
the cabins, but headed for the big steamer. When I
pushed the door of the captain's room open, I found
that it was occupied by three men who were sitting at a
table playing cards. I unloaded my pack, took off my
parka and mitts, and seated myself near the stove facing
the men. I placed my Winchester near me, took out
my pipe, and proceeded to take a smoke. As I had not
spoken to the men, they eyed me suspiciously. I had
noted that each man carried a forty-five Colt's revolver
and belt full of cartridges. A villainous-looking fellow
whose face looked familiar to me asked me where I was
from. My answer was 'Up the river.' Then I relapsed
into silence again. This appeared to anger the fellow,
who then asked me in a loud, blustering voice who I
was and what my business was down there.

I answered him quietly, saying, 'My name is Frank
Canton, Deputy United States Marshal of Alaska, and
my business is to take charge of this boat, and everything that belongs to the company who owns it.'

The three men glanced at each other. Then the big
fellow, who was evidently the leader, delivered his
ultimatum. He said, 'I guess you are out of your

latitude. There is no law in this country except what we make ourselves.' Then he went on to say that the company had contracted to take them all to Dawson last fall, but had dumped them out on this island, and caused them to lose some gold claims on the Klondike, and in order to recover damages they had seized all property that belonged to the company, that they intended to load the Cora with supplies and take her up the Koyukuk River to the mountains as soon as the ice went out, and that if I wanted to save my hide I had better keep quiet, for they intended to kill the first d—— man who interfered with them. I told him that I was awfully much obliged to him for his advice to me, but that I had always been able to take care of myself pretty well, and still thought that I could do so. Then I asked him how he expected to get possession of the Walrus.

He replied, as he dropped his hand to his hip, 'We have possession of it now.'

I was watching his move, and before either of them could draw a gun, I had them covered with my revolver and demanded that each man unbuckle his belt and pile his gun and cartridges on the table. When this was done I lined them all up against the wall and told them that I felt like shooting the whole bunch and would like to do so, but that the ground was frozen so hard that it would be a mighty cold job to dig a grave and would be still colder to cut a hole in the ice and throw them into the river. But I told them in language which I think they understood that I intended to enforce the law so long as I remained in camp, and that this was the last time that I would ever let them off. In fact I thought the best thing that I could do was to 'take the bull by the horns,' put on a bold front, and talk to them the same as if I had a company of soldiers at my back. Then I opened the door, and ordered them to file out leaving their guns on the inside. As the big fellow stepped out he gave me a look which meant trouble if he ever got the chance.

The captain soon made his appearance, but his ankle was pretty sore. When I told him of my introduction to the three men on the boat, and showed him the revolvers that I had taken, he was the best-pleased man that I ever saw, and I did not notice him limp any more from his accident. The captain had plenty of provisions on the boat and had bought some fresh black bear meat from the Indians a few days before. We soon had a good, hot supper, which I certainly enjoyed, for I was very hungry. After supper the captain told me that the men whom I had disarmed were the worst men in the camp, that these three men had taken passage at Seattle and appeared to be partners. He said the big fellow was the leader and was a most dangerous and vicious man, and that he went by the name of Tom Barkley. He said this man had organized quite a gang from a certain element in the camp and had great influence over them.

The next morning after breakfast was over I took out a United States army regulation flag that I had in my pack, unfurled it and hoisted it up over the steamer.

The news that a Deputy United States Marshal was in camp had already been circulated, but when they saw the Stars and Stripes floating over the steamer they all came out of their cabins to take a look at it. The first thing that I did was to post up written notices in conspicuous places, stating that from that date the law would be strictly enforced in camp. I then called a meeting of the people and informed them that I was representing the Department of Justice of the United States Government, and that I had heard that certain criminals in the camp had conspired to take forcible possession of the little steamer Cora, load her down with supplies to be taken from the Walrus to be used on a trip up the Koyukuk River, and that I had heard that certain thieves in the camp had stolen provisions and supplies from the steamer and sold the same to other people in the camp, and that I intended to hold the principals strictly responsible for their unlawful acts, that whenever I found a man in possession of any of the stolen supplies he would be arrested and prosecuted for receiving stolen property. However, I would say that if any man who still had any of this property in his possession would immediately return the same the captain might not prosecute them, but that it was optional with him. The next day more than a ton of the stolen supplies was returned to the steamer, for which the captain gave receipts. Barkley and his bunch were very sullen and did not attend the meeting.

The hundred and fifty passengers in this camp represented every State in America and nearly every foreign country in the world, but I found them the same as I have always found the people in every country that I have ever lived in. The majority of them was in favor of law and order, and a 'square deal,' but they were three thousand miles from civilization and not an officer in the country. Barkley and his outlaws dominated the camp, but when they found that there was a man among them who was authorized by the United States Government to enforce the laws, I found plenty of good men who would stand by me. I then appointed and swore in twenty special deputies to assist me in keeping order until we could get the steamer out of the ice and take the expedition up the river.

One evening I received information that Barkley and his two pals who lived in a cabin to themselves had some valuable furs that they had stolen off the Walrus. Early next morning I took five men over and raided their cabin. We found several silver gray fox skins, some golden marten hides, and one polar bear skin. We arrested the three men and took them over to the boat, together with the stolen furs which the captain and his purser, the clerk, identified as furs that they had bought from Esquimaux. I summoned a jury of twelve men, appointed one man to defend, and one to prosecute the prisoners, and sat as a trial judge myself. The defendants pleaded 'not guilty.' Then we proceeded with the trial which lasted all day and part of the night. The defendants were all found guilty. Barkley was fined one thousand dollars, the other two were fined five hundred dollars each, and the furs were ordered returned to the owner. As I had no place to confine the prisoners and I knew they could not escape from the island until the river broke up, I released them on their recognizance. This trial had a wholesome effect upon the community. Things began to come my way, and I found that it was not so difficult to keep order in the camp.

The history of the trial for theft of the polar bear skin was given to the Chicago 'Herald' later on by one of the passengers on the steamer Walrus who was present at the trial. He wrote a humorous article in reference to a Deputy United States Marshal on the Yukon River who arrested the criminals, summoned a jury, officiated as Judge, and approved the verdict, but he said that the defendants were given a fair and impartial trial.

It was now the latter part of April. The snow had begun to melt in the mountains, and the side streams had begun to fill with water which ran into the Yukon under the ice. This water from the large number of side streams which empty into the Yukon causes the river to rise to a tremendous flood which breaks the ice, and moves it down the river. But the Yukon proper never breaks up until about the middle of May. We had cut the ice which we found to be from five to eight feet thick around the boats, and had them anchored in clear water ready for the big smash when the river broke. I had noticed of late that Barkley was getting very restless, and every time that I looked at the fellow

I was satisfied that I had seen him before. But to save
my life I could not place him. In looking over some old
pictures of noted criminals that I had packed away,
I found a picture of a man wanted by the Governor of
Idaho, and for whom he had offered twenty-five hundred dollars reward, dead or alive. He was charged
with a vicious murder of two men and one woman by
dropping a dynamite bomb down a shaft in the Cœur
d'Alene mines in Idaho. The moment I saw the picture
I knew that it was Barkley.

The clerk of the steamer had his young wife with
him. They lived in a cabin on the point of the island,
and as she was an excellent cook, the captain and
I usually took our meals with them. The captain and
I often talked freely about our plans in the presence of
the clerk and his wife. I told them that I had discovered who Barkley was, and that when the river
broke up I intended to place him in irons and take him
up in the steamer and deliver him to the N.W.M.P. and
collect twenty-five hundred dollars from the Governor
of Idaho for his capture. I noticed that the woman was
very much interested in all that I said. I thought this
a little strange, but supposed that it was only a woman's curiosity. I would have sworn that she was perfectly loyal, for I knew that her husband was.

One evening just after dusk I came aboard the
steamer, and as I opened the front door to step in
a shot was fired from the brush on the island behind
me. A bullet crashed into the door-facing in about two
inches of my head. I first thought that I was shot in

the face, but found that I had been hit in the face by a splinter torn off the door-facing by the bullet. I sprang inside the room, and after wiping the blood off my face, I picked up my Winchester and ran outside over the gangplank and soon found moccasin tracks behind the bushes where the assassin had been lying in wait for me. I followed his trail, which was very plain where he had been running through the snow heading straight for Barkley's cabin. My first impulse was to shoot him on sight, but I wanted the reward offered for his capture, for I felt that I was entitled to it, and I still did not think that Barkley suspected that I knew his past record. I thought that the best way to handle the matter was not to make the arrest until the steamer was ready to start. From that moment I never let him get out of my sight in the daytime, and I had a friend watching his cabin at night with instructions to shoot him if he attempted to leave the island. This guard soon reported to me that the clerk's wife had several clandestine meetings with Barkley in the woods. This was a great surprise to me, when I found that the woman was in love with the outlaw. I never did think I understood women very well, but I was now willing to swear that I did not know anything about them at all. I was now satisfied that Barkley was 'on to' my game, and I felt that the sooner he was arrested the better. I said nothing to any one about the woman's attachment for the outlaw.

Large cracks had appeared in the ice on the river several days before, and without any warning the ice began to move — miles of it, slowly at first, but in less than twenty minutes the noise of acres of thick ice, bursting and jamming, sounded like the explosion of thousands of tons of dynamite. Large pieces of ice the size of an acre of land and ten feet thick would shoot out of the water onto the land and uproot big trees. Icebergs were coming down the river turning end over end. The people in the camp thought they were safe in their cabins until the river cleared, and they could get aboard the steamer, for they believed their cabins were above high water mark. They soon found the water was from three to five feet deep in the cabins, and running all over the island. Thick blocks of ice were floating down the swift current smashing cabins and trees in their path. Men and women were all fighting for their lives in the ice-cold water to push off the large blocks of ice to keep them from striking their cabins. Some of them had climbed trees for safety. We were having a hard fight ourselves to keep the heavy ice from damaging the steamer. We had given the people all of our skiffs and small boats except one lifeboat. The clerk and his wife were on top of their cabin at the point of the island in plain sight of the steamer. The water was halfway up on the sides of their cabin, and they were both calling for help. In order to rescue them we would have to row a boat out into the main channel of the Yukon to get around to their cabin at the point, which looked like suicide, for the heavy ice in the river would crush any boat like an eggshell. It was a distressing sight to see this couple calling for help on the cabin, and no way to get to them. All at once Barkley and one of his pals appeared alongside of the steamer on some logs that they had lashed together with ropes. Barkley called to me and asked if he could have a boat to go to the rescue of the clerk and his wife. I told him that he could have the lifeboat, and gave him a long pole with a spear and ice hook on one end for his partner to fight the ice floe. I believed that Barkley would do all he could to save the woman at least. They headed the lifeboat for the whirlpool of ice, and shot out into the boiling rapids. It looked like certain death. They had about one chance in a thousand to steer their boat through the swift current and get out of the ice floe. Barkley was at the oars, his partner using the pole. At times the boat appeared to be on top of an ice cake, at other times a block of ice would be driven under it throwing the boat clear out of the water. But the men held on, fighting for life, until they finally worked the boat out of the swift current into eddy water back of the island, where they made a landing near the cabin.

Barkley drove the boat up against the cabin, and while his partner held the boat against the side of the cabin by catching onto the wall, the clerk and his wife dropped off the roof into the lifeboat. As they left the cabin they looked back and saw it topple over, and the logs and household goods were floating out to the swift current of the Yukon. They pulled the boat up to another cabin on higher ground where they waited until the water receded on the island so they could get over to the steamer.

The courageous act of these men in staking their lives on what appeared to be a losing card for the rescue of the clerk and his wife was the most splendid exhibition of nerve that I ever witnessed. I could not help but feel that it was a great pity that such men should have chosen the crooked trail of crime instead of being real men among men. Only one man in camp besides myself knew what inspired Barkley, the outlaw, to take such desperate chances in the face of almost certain death to save this woman. When the first big ice floe had passed down the river the water on the island began to recede very fast, and it was not long until the ground was bare, but the island was covered with huge blocks of ice that had settled on the ground.

When the water fell the people were shivering in their wet clothes and were anxious to get aboard the steamer as quickly as possible. They had lost almost all of their supplies and bedding, but they were happy and thankful to know that they had escaped with their lives.

The river now was clearing of ice so that a boat could travel with comparative safety. I was on the island late one evening watching Barkley, for I expected him to attempt to escape that night. He still had our lifeboat tied up in the water near his cabin. After dark I took a position behind some big blocks of ice near Barkley's cabin where I could watch the lifeboat. The clerk and his wife had gone aboard the steamer. Just after dark Barkley and a woman approached and hurriedly stepped inside, leaving the door open. I recognized the clerk's wife by her voice. She was pleading with Barkley not to force her to leave her husband, saying that it would be a crime for her to do so for he had always been good to her and trusted her fully. Barkley told her that she was the only woman that he had ever loved, that he was not an outlaw, and the Marshal had lied, that the lifeboat was ready and he would take her down the river to St. Michael and then to the Pacific coast where he would marry her and make her happy. She finally promised to go. Then he told her to get certain things together for him and to wait until he took a stock of supplies, blankets, etc. to the boat, and that he would return for her in twenty minutes.

I crawled behind the ice blocks as he passed me. Then I stepped out from my hiding place and followed him cautiously until he had almost reached the boat. I approached him from behind, tapped him on the shoulder with my left hand, and ordered him to throw up his hands. As he turned he was looking into the muzzle of my revolver. I then took his revolver out of the holster at his belt. After he was disarmed I told him that I had known all the time that he was wanted in Idaho for murder, and that twenty-five hundred dollars was offered for his arrest, dead or alive, that he was now scheming to ruin a good woman, that he had tried to assassinate me, and that I thought he ought to be shot like a wolf, that I could take him up on the steamer and collect the reward for his capture, that he would have to answer to a court in Idaho for the

murder of two men and a woman, but on account of
his heroic act in saving this woman and her husband
from certain death at the risk of his own life, I intended to turn him loose and give him one more
chance to make good. He did not deny that he was
the man wanted by the Governor of Idaho. I ordered
him to take his sack of provisions and blanket roll
and get into the lifeboat. I then covered him with
my revolver and ordered him to throw out his
Winchester and one of the oars. I told him that he
could drift down the river to St. Michael, but that I intended to make sure that he would not row the bark up
the river. He threw out the rifle and oar and as I un-
tied the painter, and threw him the rope, he swore with
a bitter oath that he would get me before I left Alaska.
I watched him until the boat drifted out to the swift
current. I have never heard of him since.

It takes time to tell these things, but from the time
I left the cabin where the woman was waiting for the
outlaw, it was about thirty minutes until I returned.
Evidently she had changed her mind, for as I approached the cabin she was coming out to go back to
the steamer. When she saw me she started to run,
thinking that I was Barkley returning for her. But
when I called to her she stopped. I told her that she
would not have to fear Barkley any more, that he was
now drifting down the Yukon River in an open boat
with only one oar. She appeared to be greatly relieved
as she sobbed out her story that she had become in-
fatuated with the man and that, after she had com-

promised herself by meeting him secretly the first time, she was then in terror of him for fear that he would murder her husband and possibly herself, which he had told her that he would do unless she eloped with him. I suppose she was a good woman. I am sure that her husband thought so, but she had lost her head. I promised to keep her secret, and took her over to the steamer and soon turned in for the night.

The next morning we got all passengers aboard, took in our anchors, swung the Walrus out into the current, and started our journey. We had seen the big show, the breaking up of the Yukon, which is considered the greatest sight that a man can see in Alaska. Until a man has seen this sight he is called a 'Chechacka,' which means tenderfoot. After he has seen the river break up, he is entitled to be called a 'sour dough,' or old-timer. We found the current so swift that it was impossible to make much headway up the river. We were forced to move very slowly, although we had powerful modern machinery on the boat and plenty of wood for making steam. When we reached Rampart City, I went ashore and persuaded my old friend, Bill Painter, to go up the river with me. I intended to try to get Painter to go out that summer and return to his family in Oklahoma where he had a good comfortable home. Rex Beach drifted down the river, and I think was at Cape Nome when the discovery of gold was made. Then I lost track of him, but learned that later on he began to write short stories for magazines until he found out what he was good for. He then wrote

'The Spoilers' and 'The Barrier' and other Alaska stories which made him famous as a writer.

When we reached Circle City, which is one of the extreme northern points on the Yukon River, I parted with the captain and passengers of the Walrus. I found a big lot of mail on my arrival at Circle City. I secured a comfortable cabin for my quarters and office, and then made my first report to the Attorney General at Washington, D.C.

CHAPTER X

LIFE AT DAWSON

WHEN I reached Dawson I struck the hardest town that I had ever seen. There were about fifty thousand people there, and they were still coming in from Skagway via the Chilcoot Pass and down the Yukon River. The whole country appeared to have gone crazy with excitement and the lust for gold. The mountain passes grew black with struggling human beings, fighting, falling, rising, fighting on. It was like a blind stampede of crazed animals. Nothing could check them but exhaustion or death. Dawson grew from dozens to hundreds in a day, from hundreds to thousands. It was a wild, picturesque, lawless mining camp. The like had never been known and never will be seen again. It was a picture of blood and glittering gold dust, starvation and death. They worked all day in the mines, and danced or gambled all night. Their only passion appeared to be for women and gold. If a man could not get the woman he wanted, the man who did get her had to fight for his life. If they could not dig the gold out of the earth, they would get it in some other way. All the best tents or cabins were occupied by saloons. Every saloon had a dance hall in the back of it, and rooms for the girls. Every saloon had its gambling rooms too, unless the tables and games were all out in the open saloon. All kinds and conditions of

THE FOURTH OF JULY IN DAWSON, 1899

men and women were represented. Miners, prospectors, millionaires, adventurers, desperadoes, brave-
hearted, earnest women, dissolute dance-hall girls, and
more dangerous still, the quiet seductive adventuress.
They were all there, side by side, tent by tent, cabin by
cabin.

Almost daily new gold discoveries were made and
stampedes were pulled off. Some of the claims were on
Bonanza, Eldorado, Hanker, Gold Bottom, and other
small creeks that flow into the Klondike near Dawson.
I saw a pack train of mules coming in from the creeks
loaded down with gold dust packed in buckskin sacks
to be weighed out and deposited in the company stores
to be shipped down the Yukon and out to the States.
Many of the lucky fellows who had only from ten to
twenty thousand would take their gold dust down the
river in open boats rather than pay the high prices
charged by the companies for transporting gold dust
on the steamers. Some of the claims ran two hundred
dollars to the pan (twenty-five cents to the pan is good
pay). Whiskey sold for twelve dollars a bottle, or fifty
cents a drink. In fact nothing could be bought for less
than fifty cents. It was not uncommon for a miner
who had a good claim to blow in one thousand dollars
a night in a dance hall.

One day an enterprising young fellow drifted down
the river to Dawson and announced that he had late
newspapers from Seattle with a full account of the first
American victory at San Diego. He rented the largest
hall in the camp and charged two dollars admittance.

He had a full house and read the papers to the audience, then took them down to the river in an open boat and sold each one for two dollars. This was the first authentic news we had received relative to the Spanish American war. That night the Americans painted the town red. The N.W.M.P. and the Canadian soldiers on duty at Dawson simply turned the town over to us. They could do nothing else, for we had it anyway.

A good-looking young widow landed at Dawson one evening with a scow-load of poultry and fresh eggs, the first that had ever been seen in Alaska. She sold her eggs readily at fifty cents each. They gave her any price she asked for chickens and turkeys. I think the highest price paid for turkeys was twenty-five dollars.

Swift Water Bill, whom Jack London has mentioned in several of his Alaska stories, was there in all his glory. He had staked a claim on some of the creeks, found rich pay dirt, and sold out for one hundred thousand dollars. This was when the boom was at its height and the wildest days of the camp. Then Bill fell in love with a little black-headed Creole girl from Louisiana. After he had spent thousands of dollars on her presents, she took up with another fellow. One day Bill dropped into a restaurant and found his girl there with the other fellow eating eggs for dinner. To get even with the couple Bill contracted with the proprietor at once for all the eggs he had in stock in order to get a corner on eggs. This deal cost him twenty-five hundred dollars. He continued to blow in his money until he had spent every dollar of his fortune and could not even buy a drink on credit. He was then called 'Slow Water William.' He was a husky young fellow and had plenty of nerve. He had been in the country for several years prior to the gold discovery of 1896. He was a good traveler on snowshoes, and got his name by being an expert at shooting rapids and poling a boat up swift streams. He was now disgusted with himself, and was just waiting for a chance to get out of Dawson.

In the winter of 1908 three Russians who had just arrived in Dawson asked Bill if he knew where they could stake claims, that they wanted to prospect for gold. Bill told them that every claim in the Klondike district was staked and that the camp was full of idle men who were flat broke like himself, and no chance to get employment. This was true. He told them that he knew the country, and that if they would furnish a grubstake and a dog team he would take them where they could find good claims that would make them all rich. They accepted his proposition, got up an outfit, and the four men pulled out. Bill did not know whether he would strike anything or not. His principal object was to get away from Dawson, and the farther, the better it would suit him. But he had believed for several years that there was gold on Indian Creek over the mountains some two hundred miles from Dawson, as he had seen gold nuggets brought out of that country by the natives, so he decided to head for that section. When they reached Indian Creek they made camp and prospected some four or five weeks without

'striking a color.' Then they found decomposed quartz
which was soft and easy to work. They pulverized this
quartz by pounding it up with their trail axes and
washed it out with their gold pans. They found that it
was immensely rich in coarse gold, for they took out
several thousands of dollars' worth. Bill claimed the
discovery, which he was entitled to, and staked one
thousand feet up and down the creek. The others
staked five hundred, according to the laws of the country. There was plenty of gold for all and they were
overjoyed at their good luck.

The party now found that their supply of provisions
was almost exhausted, and what was still worse they
were having terrific snowstorms which made it impossible to get out and kill any game. In fact they soon
found themselves completely 'snowed in.' Swift Water Bill knew what this meant. He told his partners
that there was only one chance, and that was to hitch
up and pull back over the mountains, that they might
have to eat their dogs before they reached Dawson, but
to stay there meant certain death by starvation. But
the Russians were afraid that if they left some one
would come in and jump their claims and they voted
to remain in camp and take their chances. Bill took a
small piece of bacon, a few sea biscuits, put on his snowshoes, and started on his perilous journey. As he
tramped through the pine timber he used his trail axe to
blaze the trees so that he could find his way back over
the trail. After a few days he ran out of grub and was
almost starved, but he managed in some way to snare

a rabbit. This saved his life. He had a most terrible trip, but finally staggered into Dawson and was found unconscious lying on the street. He was picked up and given warm shelter, nourishment, and good treatment. When he regained consciousness he told his story in part, which created a sensation in the camp. They knew he was telling the truth, for he had a thousand dollars' worth of gold in his gold sack, and there would have been a wild stampede for claims, but Bill had not told them where the claims were located.

As soon as he got able to travel he found that he had plenty of friends. Some of the saloon-keepers who had 'turned him down' for the drinks offered to furnish him all the money he wanted, but he declined their propositions. However, he got up a party and with good dog teams and plenty of supplies, he led the party back to the camp over the trail that he had marked.

They found the skeletons of the three Russians and the bones of the dogs. The wolverines had picked the meat off the dead bodies. A sheet-iron camp kettle in the cold ashes had moccasins and pieces of dog hide that they had tried to boil, which showed that the men had actually starved to death.

After Swift Water Bill made his second big stake I was told that he saved his money and went out to San Francisco, got married, and settled down.

The North American Trading and Transportation Company at Dawson had accumulated about one million in gold dust which they wanted to ship down the river by steamer to St. Michael, and then transfer to an ocean steamer to be taken across to the mint in San Francisco. As almost the entire route was through American territory the company requested me as an American officer to take charge of the bullion down the river. This coarse gold is very heavy and troublesome to handle. It was packed in strong buckskin sacks worth about twenty-five hundred dollars each. These sacks were then securely packed down in strong wooden boxes, locked and sealed. It took twelve men to carry one of these boxes and load it on the steamer.

After we had loaded all the treasure on the steamer T. B. Weare, I selected Bill Painter and three other good men as guards to go with me. Typhoid fever had broken out in Dawson and almost every case appeared to be fatal. One of my intimate friends, who had been a passenger on the steamer Walrus and had rendered me valuable assistance in the capture of Tom Barkley, was taken suddenly ill with typhoid. I knew he had about one chance in a hundred to pull through if left in Dawson, so I got the captain to permit me to put him on the steamer, after I had found a doctor and trained nurse among the passengers and engaged them to look after my friend.

Then we left the landing at Dawson and started down the Yukon River. The current was very swift and we made good time down stream. My friend Paul Dinslee died after two days out. As I was anxious to hurry him to some settlement where white people lived, we stopped at the Holy Cross Mission down the river. I found a Catholic priest in charge. I told him that I wanted to bury my friend in his cemetery, but when I told him that my friend was a member of the Masonic Lodge he objected, saying that it was contrary to the rules of the Catholic Church to bury a Mason in a Catholic cemetery.

Fifty miles farther down the river we found the steamer Hamilton tied up for repairs with about two hundred passengers aboard. Among this number I found twenty-eight Masons besides myself and the captain. We had a deep grave dug among the flowers and green grass above high water mark, then organized our Masonic party and gave him a Masonic funeral which was very impressive, and I am sure that it was the first Masonic funeral ever held on the Yukon River.

We reached St. Michael without accident, and I delivered the gold dust to the captain of the steamer Roanoake, an ocean steamer. I felt relieved when I had a receipt in my pocket for this valuable treasure. Bill Painter took passage on the Roanoake as a guard to San Francisco. He then returned to his family in Oklahoma. I returned to Circle City where I found that I had plenty of work to keep me busy in the Marshal's office.

During the summer of 1898 and until the river closed in the fall, thousands of people from Dawson and the upper river country drifted down the Yukon in open boats in order to catch the last ocean steamer out from St. Michael to Seattle. The majority of these people were flat broke and there were some desperate characters among them. Eagle City above Circle City was the boundary line between Canada and the United States. The N.W.M.P. were kept busy handling the criminal element on the Canadian side. When outlaws escaped from the Canadian authorities and drifted down to the American side, I usually picked them up and held them at Circle City until the Canadian officers came after them, which they always did promptly. The N.W.M.P. would then return the same compliment to me by holding criminals who had escaped from the American side until I could get them down to Circle City. We dispensed with all red tape relative to requisitions and simply worked together in the interest of good government, and for the protection of honest citizens on both sides of the line. The result was that we rid the country of some very bad men.

I had selected a large cabin adjoining my office in Circle City which I had remodeled and used for a jail which I kept filled up with prisoners most of the time, although I did not hold any except the worst criminals, for the reason that we were sometimes compelled to hold our prisoners a year before we could get rid of them. Judge Crane, United States Commissioner, would commit the prisoner to jail to await the action of the grand jury at Sitka, about three thousand miles from Circle City over the water. It cost one dollar a meal to feed each prisoner, and they did their own cooking. The entire Territory of Alaska at this time was in one District and Sitka, on the southeast coast, was the capital. Judge Crane being the only United States Commissioner, and I the only Deputy United

States Marshal in the interior of Alaska, I soon found
that I had a man's job on my hands. However, I kept
up the work of my office under great difficulties until
late in the summer.

One day we heard the welcome signal of a steamboat
whistle down the river below Circle. In a short time
the steamer came in sight around a bend near the village. A bugle call was sounded under the Stars and
Stripes, and we could see the deck was crowded with
United States soldiers wearing the American uniform.
This was the most pleasant sight that I had witnessed
since I landed in Alaska, for I knew that I now had the
backing of 'Uncle Sam' in reality, and could discharge
the duties of my office without having to take my life
in my hands every minute of the time. Four hundred
soldiers landed at Circle City under command of my
old friend Lieutenant Richardson, now a general, who
went into Alaska with me in 1897. Captain Patrick
Henry Ray had gone out over the ice the winter before,
which left Lieutenant Richardson the ranking officer
in Alaska. The troops were sent in to Lieutenant
Richardson, and he was directed by the Department to
make headquarters at Circle City. There were plenty
of vacant cabins in Circle, and the officers soon had the
men in good, comfortable quarters. They had brought
in a large and excellent supply of provisions and
other supplies needed by the command. The presence
of these troops stationed at Circle City had a wholesome effect on the lawless element along the Yukon
River, and when I needed any assistance in making

arrests the commanding officer would always furnish
me a sufficient number of troops to assist me, which
took a great burden off my shoulders, and I found it
much better than having to play a 'lone hand.'

During the latter part of the winter of 1899, I had
occasion to make a trip down the river to old Fort
Yukon, which is one hundred miles below Circle City, to
arrest three outlaws whom I had wanted for some time.
I had several men in my party and two good dog teams.
It was now getting along towards spring and the warm
rays of the sun had begun to affect the snow and ice.
This was the best time of the year to travel with dog
team and sled, but it was very hard on the eyes. The
bright, warm sunshine caused a steam to rise from the
snow which would soon blind a man completely unless
he wore snow glasses. I was well aware of this danger
before I left Circle, and had provided each of my men
and myself with a pair of smoked glasses.

I found my three men in a wood camp and placed
them under arrest without any serious trouble. We all
camped in a cabin the first night. When we got ready
to take the trail next morning I found that my snow
glasses were gone. I searched the cabin and the prisoners closely but failed to find them. I knew that it
would be dangerous to attempt to make the trip without some protection for my eyes, so I decided that I
would try the Esquimo plan, which was to use burnt
charcoal and make a black mark under each eye. They
claim this will prevent one from getting snow blind. I
burned some charcoal before leaving the cabin, drew a

black mark under my eyes, and put a piece of charcoal in my pocket. However, this plan did not work in my case. In the afternoon of the first day on the trail my eyes began to itch and burn. The sensation was most unpleasant. The next day I was much worse, but kept on my feet the best I could. On the afternoon of the third day I began to suffer intensely. I felt as though needles were piercing my eyeballs, and I could see nothing. My men put me on one of the sleds and on the fourth day we reached Circle City. The prisoners were locked up, and for two weeks I remained in my cabin in almost total darkness. The United States Surgeon of the Medical Department advised me to leave Alaska as soon as possible, and go out to the States where I could get treatment for my eyes.

In the summer of 1899 I sent in my resignation as Deputy United States Marshal and took the first boat down the Yukon River via St. Michael and Cape Nome where I took passage on the steamer Cleveland, the same boat that I went in on. The second day out from the Alaska coast we ran into a tremendous storm in the Bering Sea which lasted for thirty-six hours. We had exhausted our supply of coal, and had but little ballast. The steamer was on her side about one half the time. The captain and crew had almost entirely lost control of the boat. We drifted about four hundred miles off our course, out near the coast of Japan, but fortunately for us all we kept out on the high sea. It was lucky that we were not driven onto the rugged coast. When the storm had abated and the terrific wind went down, the captain got his bearings, but the sea was now rolling worse than ever, which is always the case after a bad storm. We had two thousand bushels of wheat aboard, which was used as ballast for the boat. We burned all this wheat to make steam, and got started on our route. But in order to keep the old tub moving on our course, we were compelled to utilize nearly everything on the boat that would burn to make steam. We cut down every mast and cabin on the upper deck and tore out all wooden lining on the inside of the big steamer, and all plank floors were burned. Finally we drifted into Dutch Harbor, a coaling station on the Aleutian Islands, where we anchored for several days for repairs, and to take on a supply of coal. From Dutch Harbor to Seattle we had fair weather and a good voyage. I understand that when the steamer Cleveland made her next trip to Alaska she foundered near Unimak Pass and went to the bottom of the sea.

CHAPTER XI

BACK TO OKLAHOMA

I SUFFERED considerably with my eyes during the voyage over, on account of the bright sunshine on the water, which affected my eyes the same as the snow in Alaska, but in a short time after I went ashore I began to improve rapidly.

I remained in Seattle a short time and then went to Buffalo, Wyoming, to see my family. I found that conditions in Wyoming were very much changed since I had left there. Almost all of the large cattle owners had sold their herds and had quit the cattle business. The sheep men had taken advantage of the situation and had secured by lease or purchase most of the grazing land that had water on it, and had stocked the country with sheep. I remained with my family at Buffalo all winter, and in the spring of 1900 I returned to Pawnee, Oklahoma, where I again entered the service to hunt down outlaws.

In 1901 the Comanche and Kiowa Indian reservation in southwestern Oklahoma was opened for settlement. My old friend of Alaska, Bill Painter, had accepted a position as the first sheriff of Comanche County after the opening of the Indian reservation, with headquarters at Lawton. When this country opened up for settlement many of the loose criminal element drifted into Lawton and the town grew from a small village to a camp of more than ten thousand people in a week, and some of the toughest men in the Southwest were there — whiskey peddlers, 'three card monte men,' the 'big mit' man — and every kind of gambling fraternity was in operation in shacks and tents day and night. They also had the 'stick up' man, and the midnight murderer who was ready if necessary to cut a man's throat for twenty-five dollars. Bill Painter sent me word to come over and help him run the sheriff's office. I went on active duty as field officer in Comanche County. This was a very large county at that time, which extended clear to Red River on the southwest. The worst thieves we had to contend with in the field were horse thieves and cattle thieves, but after a good many convictions at Lawton we finally broke up the organization.

The Bert Casey gang of robbers and murderers broke out in Oklahoma while I was in Alaska, but were still operating when I returned. This was the most vicious and merciless band of young outlaws that we ever had in the country, and they murdered many good officers before they were run down. At one time they held up and robbed Dr. Beanblossom and party on the road near Rush Springs, Oklahoma, and then deliberately shot and killed a young boy, the son of Dr. Beanblossom.

Jim Thompson, the brave and efficient sheriff of Caddo County, Oklahoma, and Bill Fossett, United States Marshal, and Deputy United States Marshal Chris Madsen had been camping on the trail of these outlaws for months and finally gave them what was coming to them. Bert Casey and one of his trusted lieutenants were shot and killed by two of Bill Fossett's deputies. Marian and Perkins, two men of the gang, were captured and sentenced to life imprisonment from Lawton. This broke up the Casey gang.

Bill Painter retired from the sheriff's office and C. C. Hammond was elected sheriff of Comanche County. I still remained on duty in Comanche County until I accepted a position with the Cattle Raisers' Association of Texas to take charge of the criminal work on the range in Osage County, Oklahoma. I sent for my family and settled at Fairfax, Oklahoma.

The most troublesome and daring outlaw in Oklahoma at that time was a man by the name of Ben Cravens, who commenced his criminal career along the border of Kansas as a bootlegger, and later on he held up and robbed a store just over the line in Kansas. Finally I arrested him for stealing cattle in the Osage country, took him to Perry, Oklahoma, and delivered him to the Deputy United States Marshal Nix, in charge of the Perry jail. He was placed in jail, but in less than a week he broke jail and released all the other prisoners. Then he began robbing banks, post offices, and stores in small towns. His depredations covered almost the entire Territory of Oklahoma. He was considered the most daring outlaw in the country and for several years he was hunted by the officers like a wild animal. He had many duels with the officers in different sections of the country, but always made his escape in a running fight. He was shot at and escaped injury so many times that he appeared to have a charmed life.

Generally he had one man with him who was some reckless young fellow who would do anything that Cravens told him to do. Finally he picked up a desperate young fellow by the name of Dick Ainsley, who lived near the Sac and Fox Indian agency. Cravens and Dick planned to rob a bank at Blackwell, Oklahoma. The two outlaws first went into Blackwell and got the location of the bank which they intended to rob the next day, then bought some supplies and went out to a deserted cabin in the woods near Blackwell and made camp for the night. The officers in Blackwell had seen the two suspicious-looking men in town and after the outlaws had left, a posse was organized after dark and followed the outlaws to the cabin in the woods. The officers surrounded the cabin, and got positions where they could watch the window and door of the house until daylight to make the attack. Early next morning the outlaws by some means found that they were surrounded by armed men. Cravens decided at once to adopt his old tactics and make a running fight for the woods. The two outlaws filled their cartridge belts and magazines of their rifles full of cartridges, and both sprang out in the open firing rapidly as they ran. Dick had succeeded in getting off about forty yards when he was shot through the heart by Deputy United States Marshal Lund. Ben Cravens was shot down near the cabin; two bullets passing through his body made ugly wounds which were sup-

BEN CRAVENS

posed to be mortal. When the officers closed in on him he asked if Dick had made his escape. The officers got a wagon and team and took Cravens and the dead body of Dick Ainsley into Blackwell. Cravens refused to talk about the dead outlaw except to say that he called him Dick. This caused the officers to suspect that the dead man was the notorious Dynamite Dick, whom I had placed in the Guthrie jail several weeks before, and who had escaped with Bill Doolin and was still at large. They sent word to me to come up at once to see if I could identify him. United States Marshal Pat Nagle, Charley Colcord, and myself went to Blackwell on the first train. When I looked at the body of the dead outlaw I told the officers that Dynamite Dick was still at large, and that the dead man was Dick Ainsley. Then we entered another room where Ben Cravens was lying on a bed.

He recognized me at once, and looking straight at me, he said, 'I know you, Frank Canton. You are the d—— officer that put a bullet into the cantle of my saddle while I was on my horse one dark night in the Otoe Indian country.'

Then he began to cough and bleed at the mouth. I gave him a drink of water and asked him if there was anything I could do to relieve his suffering.

He answered, 'No. I guess they have got me this time.'

We left him, thinking that he would not live but a few hours, but to the surprise of every one he got well, and was taken to Kansas where he was tried and convicted of highway robbery, and sentenced to the penitentiary at Lansing, Kansas, for fifteen years.

After he had served for a time he was placed to work in the coal mines several hundred feet under the ground. There was also a notorious train robber by the name of Ezell who worked in the same gang with Cravens. These two men soon commenced planning an escape. They got some tools, made two wooden revolvers with long barrels, managed in some way to get a lot of tinfoil, and, by wrapping this tinfoil nicely around the wooden revolvers, they made murderous-looking weapons in the dim light at the bottom of the shaft. There was an armed guard stationed at the bottom of the shaft, but he was protected in such a way that the convicts could not get hold of him with their hands. At an opportune time Cravens and Ezell held up the guard with their fake revolvers and disarmed him. After securing his arms and ammunition, they forced him to give the signal to hoist them to the top of the shaft, then made a break for liberty right out under the guns of the guards who were shooting at the outlaws from every direction. Both of the convicts made their escape. I understand that Ezell was badly wounded, but Cravens got through without a scratch. He left his friend Ezell to paddle his own canoe, then stole a horse and was soon back in the Osage Indian country.

I heard of him when he first crossed the Kansas line. I trailed him over into his old haunts in the Otoe Indian reservation, but there lost track of him. In hunt-

ing for the trail of the outlaw I ran onto a cowboy
whom I knew. I wrote a telegram addressed to the
officers in different parts of the territory advising them
that Ben Cravens was in the country, and to be on the
watch for him. I directed the cowboy to ride to the
nearest telegraph station as quickly as possible, and
send the message. It was not long until sheriffs and
possemen were in the saddle scouring the country on
the hunt for Cravens. I found out later on that
Cravens had gone to a settlement near Kingfisher,
Oklahoma, and had induced a young farmer by the
name of Bert Welty to go with him and help him rob a
store and post office at Red Rock, Oklahoma. This
little town was located on the Otoe Reservation.

In order to avoid suspicion Cravens disguised himself
to look like a farmer. Welty put on a woman's dress
and a sun bonnet, and they rigged up a light wagon,
tied an old plough on behind, hitched their saddle
horses to the wagon and drove across the country to
Red Rock. They reached their destination about dark.
They hitched their horses in the timber, and walked
several hundred yards carrying their Winchesters in
their hands. When they entered the store they found
several people standing around. The robbers quickly
held them up and searched them. A young man by the
name of Alva Bateman, who was postmaster, had been
standing in the back of the store. When the robbers
held up the crowd he picked up a revolver and fired a
shot at one of them, but missed his aim. The two outlaws then opened fire on young Bateman, killing him

instantly. They robbed the post office of several hundred dollars and then made a break for their horses.

A heavy storm had broken loose. The rain was pouring down in torrents accompanied by terrific thunder and lightning. The outlaws had considerable trouble in finding their horses, but finally found the outfit where they had left it. After they had got into the wagon they drove the team at a breakneck speed across the prairie in an easterly direction. They soon ran into a gulch in the darkness and broke their wagon down. They took the harness off the horses and put their saddles on them. Welty had the money in a sack. Ben Cravens now showed his true character. He had induced young Welty to help him commit the crime of murder and robbery, and now had no further use for him. He pulled a shotgun out of the wagon and fired point-blank at Welty's face. Welty dropped to the ground, and Cravens, thinking that he had shot his head off, secured all the money, then mounted one horse, led the other one, and disappeared in the darkness.

Bert Welty lay in the rain where he fell for several hours, before regaining consciousness. When Cravens fired the shot the darkness saved Welty's life. He received only a part of the charge in his face, but it made a bad and dangerous wound. Welty walked some ten miles to Black Bear Creek and went to the home of a farmer by the name of Hetherington whose place was a 'hold-out' for Ben Cravens in former days. This farmer got a doctor, who cared for Welty until he got better. The officers at Perry, Oklahoma, went out to Hetherington's place and arrested Welty, who later on was convicted and sentenced to life imprisonment for the murder of Alva Bateman.

The officers at Perry had been notified immediately after the murder and robbery at Red Rock and some of them had reached Red Rock the same night. Early the next morning Jean Branson, a deputy sheriff from Perry, struck the trail of the robbers. The heavy rain the night before had made the ground very muddy and it was no trouble to follow the trail of the two horses which led due east in the direction of the town of Pawnee. Branson followed the trail to within a few miles of Pawnee and found the tracks led up to a farmer's house. The farmer's name was Cunningham. The officer, keeping under cover himself, saw two horses in the corral, that appeared to have been ridden hard recently. Thinking that both outlaws were in the house he went to Pawnee, and got the sheriff and a posse to assist him. When they returned they surrounded the house, then called Cunningham out and questioned him as to who was in the house. He denied that Cravens was there. While this parley with Cunningham was going on, Tom Johnson, a deputy sheriff from Pawnee, took a position in the open about ten feet from the front door. Evidently Ben Cravens could see the officer. He pushed the front door open with the muzzle of his high-powered rifle, and as quick as lightning shot Tom Johnson down, giving him a mortal wound.

Cravens then sprang out of the door and made a run
across an open field over plowed ground for about
eighty yards, then jumped over a bluff into a ravine and
got away. This was a remarkable escape, for it was in
broad daylight and they were all shooting at him at
close range. Sheriff John Chrisman was a good shot,
and his deputy Joe Weariman was an expert rifleman.
They had good positions and both emptied the magazines of their rifles, but the outlaw escaped without a
scratch.

For the next four or five years every officer in the
Territory was on the lookout for Ben Cravens. Rewards
were offered for him, and he was the most-talked-of
outlaw that had ever been in the country. He was
accused of nearly every hold-up and other notorious
crime committed in Oklahoma, when the criminals
were not captured or killed; none of which reports were
true. He was reported to have been seen in Texas, Old
Mexico, Arizona, and New Mexico. I have had men
whom I would have sworn were honest, truthful men
tell me that they knew Ben Cravens and had seen him
at different points, but after I had investigated these
reports I found that without any question of doubt
there was not a word of truth in any of them. Cravens
had disappeared as completely as though he had been
swallowed up by an earthquake.

It was a mystery to me as well as many other officers,
but the mystery was cleared up several years later.
What Ben Cravens actually did was this. After he had
killed Tom Johnson near Pawnee and escaped I pre-

sume some of his friends on Black Bear Creek furnished
him a saddle horse, for we never heard of a horse being
stolen. Cravens then went to Missouri and hired out as
a hand to do farm work. He continued to work on a
farm for several years under the name of Charley
Maust, and was considered an honest, hard-working
fellow. He got married under the name of Maust, and
his wife worked on a farm with him. He finally stole a
horse and was convicted and sentenced to serve three
years in the pententiary at Jefferson City, Missouri.
One day while in the Missouri penitentiary, he was
recognized by a barber who had been in the Lansing,
Kansas, penitentiary with him. This barber informed
the officers at Jefferson City who the convict Maust
really was. The officers then sent to Lansing, Kansas,
and got a copy of the Bertillon record of Ben Cravens,
which they compared with that of Charley Maust. The
records were identically the same, including finger-
prints and every scar from gunshot wounds. They
notified the authorities of Oklahoma that they had
Ben Cravens who was wanted for murder in Oklahoma. Ben Cravens was then brought to Guthrie,
and tried in the United States Court before Judge
Cottrell for the murder of Alva Bateman on an Indian
reservation. John Embry prosecuted Cravens and
Al Jennings defended. I was summoned as a witness
to identify Cravens. Bert Welty was also brought
from the 'pen' and placed on the witness stand against
Cravens. Welty made a full confession of the whole
matter. The evidence for the prosecution was com-

plete and Cravens was convicted and sentenced to life imprisonment in the penitentiary at Leavenworth, Kansas. He pleaded not guilty and never admitted that his name was Ben Cravens.

The population of the Territory of Oklahoma had increased so rapidly that the people were clamoring to be admitted into the Union as a State. On June 16, 1906, the Enabling Act was passed, authorizing Oklahoma to become a State. In November, 1906, the Constitutional Convention of Oklahoma convened to frame a constitution for the government of the State. In the fall of 1907 a general election was held and C. N. Haskell was elected Governor. On the sixteenth day of November, 1907, he was inaugurated as Governor and his first official act was to appoint me Adjutant General of the new State. I had never had a great deal of military training, but I had had some, and knew in a general way what the duties of the Adjutant General were, and believed that I could render the State valuable service. Therefore I accepted the position. I moved my family to Guthrie, the capital, and entered upon the discharge of my military duties, succeeding General Alva J. Niles.

The National Guard of Oklahoma at that time consisted of one regiment of infantry. At least there was supposed to be a regiment, but I found that it was only a skeleton organization of about six hundred poorly equipped men with Roy V. Hoffman as Colonel. The National Guard, or militia, as it was formerly called,

GENERAL CANTON IN 1910

never did amount to much until Congress passed the
Dick Bill in 1903, which provided that the General
Government should furnish the National Guard all
arms and equipment and pay them a *per diem* when
called out for duty by the Secretary of War. The passage of the Dick Bill was the first step ever taken by
the United States Government to increase the efficiency
of the National Guard. The bill had a provision that
this equipment and fund should not be furnished the
several States unless the National Guard of each
State should conform to a certain standard of efficiency,
which was fixed by the War Department and passed
upon by the United States Inspectors, sent out by the
War Department to see that each National Guard
unit complied with the rulings of the War Department
relative to the standard of efficiency required.

The legislature of each State was supposed to ap-
propriate sufficient funds for armory rent, construction
of rifle ranges, especially of troops when ordered out for
drill. The State was also to pay the troops and furnish
subsistence when ordered out by the Governor to sup-
press local troubles, etc. After looking over the situation of the guard from every angle, I realized that I had
a man-sized job on my hands to build up the organization to a twelve-company regiment and meet the
standard of efficiency required by the Secretary of War.

The first thing to do was to have the legislature,
which was then in session, make sufficient appropria-
tions for the maintenance and training of the National
Guard. I found this a very difficult task. The Na-

tional Guard and the regular army at that time were unpopular with the masses of the people of the Nation for the reason that we had been at peace so long that they could not see the necessity of training the young men of the Nation for war. They seemed to think it was a useless expenditure of funds, and every time that my appropriation bill for the military department was brought up in the legislature it was fought bitterly by a certain element of politicians in the legislature. However, I always found some good, patriotic men in the legislature who were not so thick-headed and stupid, who could see far enough ahead to know that the country was likely to need trained soldiers at some time in the future to defend the Nation.

After Statehood they threw their influence and strength on my side, and with the help that I received from the officers and men of the National Guard we finally, after six months' hard work, won our fight by two votes, although they cut our appropriation bill to the minimum. I had requested to be authorized to organize two regiments, one on the east side and one on the west side of the State, but they would only allow one regiment and refused to allow the officers and enlisted men their actual expenses when they were ordered out to weekly drill. I had at least secured a sufficient State appropriation for the military department to begin to reorganize the National Guard of Oklahoma. I made requisition on the War Department for sufficient equipment to equip the regiment to full place strength, and for the next two years was very busy.

CONCLUSION

IT is to be regretted that General Canton here closes so abruptly his autobiography. There yet remained nine years of active service as commander of the Oklahoma National Guard, and these were years of achievement not unmixed with romance and adventure. His energy and enthusiasm brought the National Guard of Oklahoma up to a high point of efficiency and made of it that splendid fighting machine which was to render such valuable service in the Great War.

Excellent as was his work in building a military machine, this was but a small part of his work for the welfare of Oklahoma. Almost single-handed he put down the so-called 'Crazy Snake Uprising.' Almost single-handed he quelled 'County Seat Wars,' while fire, flood, tornado, or other disaster always brought to the scene General Canton and a few of his troopers to care for the wounded, bury the dead, protect property, and help the stricken community in every possible way.

The story of these achievements could be written from the letters, clippings, and other material among his private papers, but it has not seemed wise to do so. His life story is his own story, and he has told simply and well of its most interesting and picturesque phases. It does not seem fitting that another should attempt to add anything to such a remarkable life history.

THE END